Modern Primitive Arts

OF MEXICO, GUATEMALA AND
THE SOUTHWEST

In beauty I walk
With beauty before me may I walk
With beauty behind me may I walk
My voice restore for me
Make beautiful my voice
Make it flow in gladness
Like the warbling birds who sing in gladness.

May the children of Earth be restored in beauty

Before me beautiful
Behind me beautiful
Over me beautiful
Under me beautiful
All around me beautiful
Everlasting and Peaceful

NAVAHO CHANT

MODERN
PRIMITIVE ARTS

OF MEXICO, GUATEMALA AND

THE SOUTHWEST

by Catharine Oglesby

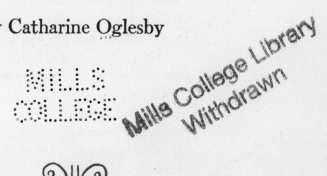

NEW YORK   WHITTLESEY HOUSE   LONDON

McGRAW-HILL BOOK COMPANY, INC.

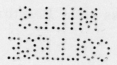

PUBLISHED BY WHITTLESEY HOUSE
A division of the McGraw-Hill Book Company, Inc.

Printed in the United States of America by H. Wolff, New York

Dedicated
in admiration and affection to
LILLIAN SEFTON DODGE
who truly
"walks in the Beautiful Way"

Contents

H. *Armstrong Roberts*

SUSANNE, PRIZE POTTER OF SAN ILDEFONSO

The potters of the pueblos never use the wheel. The pots are built by
the coil method, which we see illustrated here by Susanne, one of the
finest potters of San Ildefonso.

H. Armstrong Roberts

THE PUEBLO POTTER

Two pebbles, oftentimes heirlooms, which long use has made as brilliant as gems, are used to polish the pottery to a beautiful luster.

A DECORATOR OF POTTERY

Some men are becoming interested in pottery and are proving accomplished decorators of it. One of the most talented is José Aguilar, who here is seen inspecting the coiling serpent with which he has just decorated this corn bowl.

H. Armstrong Roberts

A POTTER OF COCHITI

At Cochiti, and other pueblos too, little apprentices take their first lesson in decorating pottery at an early age. A yucca twig, split and chewed to desired size and pliability, is used to paint on the decorations.

A PUEBLO BASKETMAKER

With only a few twigs and grasses these amazing hands fashion beautiful
baskets for use in the home and in the colorful Indian ceremonies.

H. Armstrong Roberts

A NAVAHO SPINNER

The crude distaff used by the squaw demands perfect coordination of hand and implement. It is a graceful art that literally wears the fingers to the bone.

H. Armstrong Roberts

THE NAVAHO WEAVER

The Navaho woman weaves the blankets on a crude upright loom that
has not changed in four hundred years.

THE NAVAHO SILVERSMITH

"The silver runs like a song." With crude tools the Navaho fashions silver and turquoise jewelry of distinctive design and fine craftsmanship.

A TARASCAN LACQUER ARTIST

Her ancestors invented this painting on wood, "the lacquer being so
constant that it rivals the object in duration and permanence."

H. Armstrong Roberts

DRYING TULE FOR BASKETS

When drying the tule, or reed, with which baskets are woven, the Indian
of Mexico makes lovely patterns on the grass.

A WEAVER OF CHICHICASTENANGO

Women tie a couple of poles to a handy tree and, squatting on the earth,
weave textiles that fine machines cannot duplicate.

Dorothy Connable

MAKING BASKETRY IN THE MARKET

Children and adults dress alike in Guatemala and their brown fingers
are never idle; even at the market they never cease working.

Modern Primitive Arts

OF MEXICO, GUATEMALA AND
THE SOUTHWEST

Beads *versus* Buttonholes

LIKE a little brown hen among a flock of peacocks, a small earth-colored package lay among my Christmas presents beneath the tree. They were wrapped in crisp cellophane and shining foil, tied with a multitude of bright colored ribbons, starred with gay metallic seals, save for this one little brown package. The marks of much use were on its creased Manila wrapping. Its string had been knotted many times. Yet above all the other presents it challenged my curiosity. I opened it first. There, resting in a bed of alfalfa, was a tiny black pottery horse. On its chest was etched the word "Severa".

Quick as a star-twinkle, my mind flew out of the window of my New York apartment westward, far westward. Across mountain, plain, river, prairie, desert.

Then, stronger than the scent of Christmas greens, my nostrils caught the odor of sage and sand; the crisp, pungent, acrid smell of Indian country. Brighter than the Christmas lights came the memory of the prodigal color of that far-off land. The limitless blue of the sky; deep green of cedar and pine; the brown of the earth; the mahogany hills; the fawn-colored huts, hung with strings of scarlet chili and maroon maize; foaming white streams plunging down obsidian chasms; and over all, the liquid gold of the sun—Indian country.

This little pottery pony was not merely a toy; it was an invitation. For untold ages the Indian way to say "come to see me" has been to send a horse, or a picture of a horse, to the prospective guest. Severa, daughter of the Tewa, was inviting me to visit her pueblo at Santa Clara, New Mexico, reminding me, in her quiet, humorous way, of my oft-repeated promise to come and make pottery with her.

On my last visit she had even promised to let me use her polishing stone—a smooth, black spheroid made bright as a jewel by rubbing on clay by several generations. Severa does not know how old this prized pebble is; neither did her great-grandmother. And now comes the little pottery horse urging me to visit her. A day's flight from New York—from sunup to sundown—and I could be in the land of Indian art. The temptation was too strong to be resisted.

The lovely things made by the Indians have fascinated me since I was a child. However, it took a French woman

4

to make me realize that in them was a great art. It happened this way.

I was raised in a convent on the border of what was known as Indian Territory—now called Oklahoma. Many Indian girls attended this same school. And how we superior white children loved to tease them when they arrived! We would concoct tales such as, "Radiators are instruments of torture devised by the nuns to punish bad children. When we misbehave or do not know our lessons, the nuns make us sit on them and turn on the heat." So the stories ran, but the Indian girls were too keen to believe them for long. And Indians have a gay sense of humor, despite their proverbial stolidity and dignity. So despite these mischievous introductions friendships were formed that have continued through these years and resulted in many happy holidays spent in the Indian country.

As a child, the gay colors and direct designs of their beads, bracelets, baskets and blankets attracted me. I learned to make necklaces, belts, bracelets of beads under the guidance of their sensitive brown hands and gentle dark eyes. And how regretfully the nuns would shake their heads at my preference for making beadwork to mending buttonholes!

Then it was rumored among my classmates that I was "part Indian." My olive complexion, dark eyes and black hair were sure proof that their gossip was true, so the story went. Finally it reached my ears, and I was delighted. That evening, when my mother and father came

5

to my nursery for their usual good night visit, I surprised them with the question: "Who are my real parents?"

Though they emphatically denied the rumors of my classmates, my ambitions were not to be so easily quieted. Didn't I have dark eyes? And skin? And hair? Didn't I hate to wear union suits? Didn't I adore red?

One of my favorite amusements was to comb the long, black silky hair of Juanita, a beautiful Osage girl who was my nurse. Through the long, hot afternoons she would let me comb and arrange her hair, which fell past her knees, meanwhile relating the legends of her tribe. We played that we were sisters. But my yearnings to be one with this other race came to an abrupt close.

A tribe of Indians was being moved from Louisiana to Indian Territory. They changed trains in the little town we lived in. It was the first tragedy I ever witnessed. All through one hot day—and Texas thermometers have a way of mounting to 110, 112 and 113 degrees in July shade—the little tribe waited at the station for the train coming to take them from their home to an unknown land.

The squaws sat in a half circle, their babies on their knees, the children squatting before them. An Indian stood behind his squaw. Their clothes were brilliant reds, magentas, pinks, blues. Their hair was braided, and twisted among the plaits were strands of bright beads. The shirts the men wore defied the flaming colors of tropical flowers. But there was no gaiety in their faces. Silent, patient, tragic, they waited the coming train.

The news of the passing of this picturesque tribe soon flashed through the town. In twos and threes the white people came to see the sight. Imagine the horror of my circumspect mother and father when they saw me calmly sitting on the brick sidewalk cuddling a papoose.

It was a spanking and no supper and bed at six that night. My only comfort was a little doll made of a rabbit's foot and beads and deerskin, given me by a sympathetic squaw. To this day I have that doll.

Later I was sent to a convent in the East. As I grew older, life whirled me far away from the Indian country, and I forgot about it, until one day I was invited to dinner in a sumptuous home in Paris. When the maid ushered me into a little *salon* where I might remove my wraps, imagine my surprise at finding the walls covered with Indian beadwork! Navaho rugs were on the floor, Hopi pottery carefully locked in the wall cases. At that moment, the old fascination of these simple, beautiful crafts returned. But I saw them in a new light. In Indian crafts a great art lives, but I had to cross the ocean to a foreign land to realize it. It was with mixed feelings of pride and shame that I listened that evening to the art of the American Indian discussed—in *French*.

The next few years found me visiting Indian villages from the Atlantic to the Pacific, from Canada to Panama. But I was not alone. Americans in increasing numbers were coming to an appreciation of the primitive art of the Americas that lives today in hundreds of sun-drenched villages on the Great Plateau.

CHAPTER ONE

Modern Primitive Arts of the Great Plateau

THE primitive arts of the Indian still flourish in amazing fertility along the Great Plateau. Despite the overlay of a materialistic and mechanized civilization, beautiful objects and textiles are now being made by methods centuries old along the length of this lean, rocky, arid elevation. This spine-like ridge begins to rise just south of the Rocky Mountains in New Mexico and Arizona and extends through the length of Mexico, loses itself in swampy jungles, then rears to higher and final heights in the little republic of Guatemala. On this height in pre-conquest times, there flowered a culture of unique distinction characterized by one of the most noble expressions of beauty that the world has ever known. Then suddenly a foreign civilization came, and because it knew steel and gunpowder, the Indian was despoiled, conquered, his finer culture ravaged. But the artistry of the defeated Indian rose invincible, like the legendary phoenix, and remains supreme to this day.

Though the Great Plateau is divided governmentally into three distinct parts—New Mexico and Arizona, Mexico, Guatemala—each inhabited by peoples speaking a different language and having different characteristics, they all possess three identical aboriginal arts which they still carry on. These arts are weaving, pottery and basketry. The Indians developed these arts to a high degree of perfection by methods distinctly their own. In addition, a beautiful lacquer was produced in certain parts of Mexico. Its beauty thrilled the padres in the sixteenth century, and it remains unique to this day, one of the most beautiful of modern primitive arts. On the northern stretches of the plateau another distinctive craft developed among the Navahos, that of silverwork. It is the one primitive art that has improved with time.

Methods of making have not changed in four hundred years! The women still squat on the earth and weave upon an upright loom, exactly as Cortez saw them do. Only the men in Mexico have accepted the horizontal loom, an innovation of the Spaniards. To this day, the wheel is never used by potters except in certain factories in such commercial craft centers as Oaxaca and Puebla, in Mexico. The potters working in their own villages on their own thresholds remain true to the ancient methods of shaping by hand. Basketry has not changed except in the acceptance of aniline dyes for decoration, and the magnificent lacquer of Mexico continues, in method of manufacture, exactly as of old.

Though these popular arts and their methods of making are identical except in the case of silver and of lacquer, you can come to know at first sight the exact locale in which every pot, blanket or basket produced on the plateau is made. Each of the products of the three countries has its characteristic shapes, motifs and even colors.

Consider their pottery, for instance. In Mexico, the use of three legs on the pots is as characteristic as are the serrated edges of the pots made by the Pueblos. The motifs which the Pueblos and the Indians of Mexico weave into their blankets and zerapes are rigidly geometrical. In Guatemala scores of little animals and birds— turkeys, chickens, deer, rabbits and sometimes the figures of men and women—are wondrously combined with stripes, squares, diamonds in the design of the fabrics. In this country, too, they make a gorgeous purple dye from a mollusk that the Indians in the lands toward the north never know.

Though their arts are identical, each of the three groups expresses itself in ways distinctly characteristic. The Pueblo woman is possessor of the home, where the husband is but a guest who may remain only until she chooses to wrap his belongings in a bundle and set it on a doorstep. This woman excels in making articles to use in

11

the home—blankets, pottery, baskets. Her industry, dexterity and imagination transform things of practical use into objects of rare beauty. The Indian of Mexico, gay, fanciful, irresponsible, whose home is a source of little pride, but who, cherishing fun and the fiesta, makes something charming out of everything and anything. He lavishes his genius on the merest toy no less than on the zerape to keep him warm. There is no end to the lovely things he makes. The Guatemalans, a proud, formal, quiet people, reserve their ingenuity and skill chiefly for one art—textiles, which they wear with all the grandeur of born aristocrats. There is no other country in the world today whose native costumes possess such medieval opulence of color and design as do those of the Guatemalans. And so it is that the three groups, creating identical arts in similar crude ways, interpret their own culture pattern.

To a home-loving people these Indian arts are easily understandable. For their roots are embedded deep in the desire to make the home a more beautiful place in which to live. That is their reason for being.

> *May it be delightful, my house*
> *From my head to my feet, may it be delightful*
> *Where I lie may it be delightful*
> *All above me may it be delightful*
> *All around me may it be delightful*
>
> *May it be delightful and well, my fire*
> *May it be delightful as I walk about my house*

All my possessions well may they be made
Before me may it be delightful
Behind me may it be delightful
Around, below, above me may it be delightful
All universally, may it be delightful
May the path of the sun lead ever and always
In peace to my house.

So runs the old Navaho chant, and it sounds the key to the purpose and meaning of Indian art—its inevitability.

There were beans and maize to be stored for the winter. So one day an Indian woman set about making a basket in which to store them with the materials at hand —reeds, raffia, palm fronds, yucca. And as she wove the strands in and out, she recorded in color and in texture the designs that she saw about her—birds, lightning, horses, sun, clouds. The result was a thing of beauty.

A woman was not content to cook in a pot made of dull-colored earth. With careful hands she molded the clay into a beautiful shape. With a piece of yucca or mesquite she drew lovely designs on it; sometimes in color, sometimes she merely etched on the surface a lacelike design in light and shade.

A woman wove strands of wool across the loom. She took pride in pressing them tightly and more tightly together. Thus, there was created a soft texture that made the blanket fold more gently about the body of the man she loved.

She dipped her yarns in juices and waters to give them color. She frayed out cloth she bought from traders and got more brilliant reds for her blankets. The sun, the birds, the lovely things that lived about her were drawn into the blanket with these colored strands.

The gourds that grew behind her hut were good to hold water and food. But that was not enough. So with colorings made from berries and flowers and herbs, she painted these gourds with replicas of things she considered beautiful—flowers, birds, animals, reptiles.

Thus the Indian woman evinces the primitive urge of all women to make something beautiful with their fingers and by so doing to infuse beauty into everyday life. This has been woman's great gift in the evolution of culture through the ages. Far greater than those things won by the fists of man are the achievements of the fingers of woman.

I challenge one who is a homemaker to watch an Indian weaving a blanket to keep her man warm and dry, or to watch brown hands patting, molding, polishing a jug to bring water from the spring, or to watch nimble, sensitive fingers weave the yucca, raffia or fern frond into a basket for the storing of corn for the winter, without coming to a close knowledge and sincere appreciation of Indian art. Its purpose is to make the home a more beautiful place in which to live. The wonder is that this semibarbaric race, clinging to their ancient customs for four centuries, have through their industry, deftness and taste, lightened by a fine imagination, created with simple tools and the crude materials at hand, *beauty that is rare.*

Indian art is simple, functional, and above all *alive.* It is made not only to be viewed in museums and mansions, but to be sold in the market place, to be used in the kitchen, to decorate the home. You must borrow a volume from the library to read about the creators of Italian primitives, the laughing cavaliers of Hals, the rosy nudes of Rubens, the personages of Rembrandt's portraits, but you can sit down on the warm earth, bask in the sun and actually watch brown hands mold lovely bits of pottery, weave beautiful blankets on their crude looms, convert a lowly gourd into a flowery bowl, a bit of metal into a piece of jewelry a king might wear with pride. That lovely bit of pottery you saw in the market place will go to hold beans in a hut down the road if you don't buy it for a vase for your home or apartment. That soft, colorful zerape will serve to keep some Indian warm and dry while he tends his sheep if you don't drape it over your studio couch. Indian art is alive and democratic.

You need not know the intricacies of brush strokes or chiaroscuro to discuss Indian art. It is not reserved to the effete atmosphere of the salon tea and art gallery. You walk down the road to market, and there in the sunshine, in the clear, crisp mountain air, you discuss the basket with its maker, the zerape with its weaver, the jug with its potter. Always you meet courtesy, responsiveness and oftentimes gay humor.

"That is a pretty bowl," you say. And the Indian of

New Mexico will lift it from the ground, turn it from side to side in a sensitive hand, gaze at it silently, admiringly, with gentle brown eyes, much as a jeweler turns a gem to let you see its brilliance and the purity of its color.

"That is a lovely zerape," you say, pointing to one on the bottom of the pile.

"*Si, si, señora,*" the Indian of Mexico will eagerly agree. Quick as a flash he will flit it before you, his eyes glowing, his face all smiles. "Look how beautiful! Look how cheap!"

No aura surrounds Indian art. Yet I shall never forget the expressive drop of Maria Martinez' eyelids—Maria is the master potter of San Ildefonso, and her lovely black jugs and bowls are in many prized collections—when the editor of an eastern fashion magazine stood before one of her bowls and exclaimed, "How *chic!*" Not a word, not a change of expression. Just dropped eyelids. They said much!

There is a belief that Indian art is deteriorating. Yet at the moment I write, in some pueblo in the shadow of a mountain, in many a mud hut basking under a tropical sun, a thing of beauty has come to completion.

It is true, of course, that not all Indian artists are equally gifted and, as with all artists, that not every work is equally good. If you want to buy, it is wisest to know the characteristics of the best. How can you tell? How can you separate the wheat from the chaff? I once asked a famous connoisseur of jade these same questions. His reply answers this one, too. It was:

16

"A good piece speaks to you. Stand silently before it and listen carefully. To train your ears to hear you must surround yourself only with the good. My father taught me to appreciate jade. We spent hours and hours looking at fine jade in museums and in shops. On my way home my father would ask, 'What do you remember about that cup, or bowl, or ornament?' I would try to express my observations. Then later we would spend many hours looking at inferior jade. On the way home he would ask the same question, and I would endeavor to phrase my thoughts. So I grew to learn fine jade from poor jade. But I still have much to learn!"

Today, fine specimens of Indian art have been gathered together in many museums in New York City, in Brooklyn, in Newark, in Santa Fé, in New Orleans, in Mexico City and in the department stores and shops in cities from coast to coast. You can visit them at no cost at all and thus become familiar with the marks of distinction that characterize good basketry, blankets, pottery, silver and lacquer. But the pleasantest way is to go to the Indian country. There you can chat with the Indian traders and the owners of good shops. These dealers know, not only the art, but the makers. Listen to them. And if you have little money to spend and want something fine, go to the *best* shop. If you have little money and want the fun of spending it, change a five-dollar bill into quarters and go out into the market place and buy—buy—buy. One of the delights of popular Indian art is its cheapness; you can get so much for so little. And there's no fun like spending money!

However, every art has its characteristics of quality. So come with me to market, to station, to roadside, to patio, to shop. I'll try to pass along "tips" to help you select the useful, the beautiful and the best among the gay pageant of blankets, baskets, pottery, silverwork that await your choice. Of course, I am not an authority. I am just a woman who likes beauty about me and who has been privileged to live long among the artists of the plateau. But we shall speak with experts on our way, and we shall sit in the sand and squat in the market place with the makers themselves and look and listen and maybe learn. We shall turn back Time four centuries. We shall "walk in beauty."

PART ONE

THE TRIBAL ARTS OF THE

PUEBLO AND NAVAHO

POTTERY
BASKETRY—WEAVING
SILVERWORK

CHAPTER TWO

Adobe Country

WHEN you come to the Indian country you are in the domain of sky, earth, sun and, in season, rain. But it is not like the circumscribed eastern rain. This is an eager rain that flings itself in passionate abandonment into the parched earth. Down, down, it seeps until every grain of sand is swollen, saturated, with this seminal fluid. After its coming, the earth, once dried and barren, conceives, blooms, bears, in a wealth of fertility. For the reason that the arts have flourished here for these many thousands of years is answered by one word—food.

This is the land of corn. The yellow-skinned, black-haired, slant-eyed Mongolians who followed buffalo, bison, sloth, down from the north, found corn here. And they remained. It is likely that at that time there were forests toward the north that made this a kindlier land. When they were stripped away perhaps the climate changed. Now this high, bare triangle, four thousand feet above the desert, that arches itself like a mad cat's back across New Mexico and Arizona, knows burning heat, cold winds, ravaging storms, glaring skies, torrential rains. The earth itself is sun-scorched to the colors of flame—red, yellow, orange.

The only trees are twisted pines, yucca, sage, juniper, scrub pine, greasewood, scraggling mesquite, and occasionally tall cottonwoods fringe the *café-au-lait* rivers. Springs are withered, parched. The arroyos are dry except in the rainy season. Then the floods rush through them like beasts unleashed. But the corn still grows in the fields out beyond adobe huts that bake in the sun or steam in the rain.

It is told by the old folks that the prehistoric Kisani brought the first ear of corn here from the lower world. He showed the ear to the Pueblos, and they immediately wanted some of it. Kisani agreed to break the ear in the middle and give them either end. While the Pueblos debated which end they preferred, the mischievous coyotes ran away with the tip end and left the Pueblos the butt end. And that is the reason why their corn is superior to all other kinds.

The first people to settle on this northern end of the Great Plateau, which is really the end of the Rocky Mountains and extends downward through Mexico and

Guatemala to the isthmus, are now termed the Basket Makers, so named because their graves are filled with countless baskets. Little is known of them except that they lived and passed away. After them came the tribes now living in the pueblos, and each one has a fantastic legend to explain its coming.

The Hopis say they came from underground, that they once lived in the lowest of the four worlds. Led by the war god, they traveled up and up. When they arrived at the surface of the earth, the war god permitted them to plant corn, and they have remained here ever since.

The Navahos say that they wandered down from the north; the Taosans declare that they followed a bird up from the south. When the trees knew the first spring, when the rivers trembled in their new channels, then, like fledglings in their course, the Zuñi came to the young earth to find their home. They wandered over the land until they came to the Center of the Earth. There they made their home. Today we know this great Center as a few pueblos on the fringe of New Mexico's southern border.

When the Pueblo people came, they knew bow and arrow, masonry and agriculture. They lived in one-room stone houses and practiced their religion in underground chambers. They grew numerous. In the twelfth and thirteenth centuries they built large and populous cities.

These cities were of two types. Some were cliff dwellings dug into the face of the canyon or into the side of a precipice hundreds of feet above the valley. Each pueblo had its underground ceremonial chamber, or kiva, which was carved out of the stone, no matter how hard the formation, and was entered by a ladder through a hatchway. These deserted cliff cities invariably face the southeast, and it is pleasant to sit on their ledge in the early morning sunshine and muse over the busy life they once knew.

Other pueblo cities were scarcely different from the cities we live in today. Great apartment houses, several stories high, were built along a semicircular wall. They were terraced inward, with the exterior well planned for fortification. These cities, too, had their kivas dug deep down between the banks of terraced houses.

Why did these gifted people choose to live so far from their cornfields and their water supply? Were these cities really fortifications to preserve the inhabitants from a marauding enemy? Why did their descendants forsake these safe cities to build homes down in the valley by the rivers? Science has not yet solved the mystery, but the old padres who came up from Mexico with the Spaniards had a ready answer even then.

It was all very clear, easily explained. God knew that the padres were coming. He sent the Indians down from the cliffs to settle by the rivers so that they might more surely be found and baptized.

When the Spaniards, urged by the fabulous legends of the Seven Cities of Cibola, came hunting gold in 1540, the culture of the Pueblos had already begun to decline. Whether the cause was war, famine or merely the seemingly inevitable senescence of a race, no one knows. These conquistadors found in some fifty villages a peaceful and prosperous people. They were permanently settled in homes of a distinctive type of architecture. They practiced a diversified form of agriculture and enjoyed a stable, democratic form of government. The equality of woman was recognized and monogamy practiced. Their brown hands had then the same amazing skill that still fills with wonder those who travel there today, and their arts were well developed.

Like their southern kinsmen in Mexico the Pueblos were deeply religious, but their religion called for no human sacrifice. It was highly organized, with a formal and ceremonious ritual in which every member of the tribe took part. Theirs was a religion of fertility in which the forces of nature were personalized and in which the dance and the costume played a conspicuous part. It inculcated a close kinship with animals, especially those that had a connection with rain—the snake, frog, eagle, butterfly. The deer and buffalo which furnished food and warmth, were also included, but Rain was the first god. Their religion, though intensely and wholesomely spiritual, was essentially a religion of earth, growth, fertility, life. It shocked the padres, but it consoles the Indian to this day.

The Spaniards brought the Pueblos a new religion, which they did not want, but they also brought them beans, peas, melons, cabbages, onions, peppers, peaches, wheat, horses, sheep, goats, an oven shaped like a beehive and chimneys, which they did want. The Indians accepted these gifts publicly and continued to follow their religion secretly. Then in 1630 came rebellion.

It started among the Pueblo people along the Rio Grande del Norte. Then the Zuñi to the south, the Navahos to the west, even the Hopi, isolated on their high mesas, joined. But the news leaked out. The Spaniards prepared, conquered.

In 1821 the Pueblos became a part of Spain, and governors were appointed to rule them. In 1848 the territory was taken over by the United States, but not much was done about it. When the attention of Abraham Lincoln was attracted to these strange new wards, he sent canes to the Indian governors appointed to rule the Pueblos. Today these canes may be seen in the houses of the current governors. I saw one decorated with parrot feathers hanging on a wall in Taos between pictures of the Virgin Mary and Mr. Lincoln. Outside, mass having ended, the statue of the Virgin had been placed before the door of the church while the Indians danced before her in a plea for corn, just as they had done hundreds of years before the coming of the padres who introduced Our Lady to these brown believers with ancient ways.

There was a time when Taos was the gateway to this Pueblo country. Situated at the foot of the Taos Mountains, it marked the end of a narrow pass that led directly to the plains. When Hernando de Alvarado came here in 1540, there were more than fifteen thousand people living in the terraced houses that face each other on both sides of the little Taos River which flows through the center of the town. Today there are less than five hundred.

The Taos pass is no longer used. Now airplanes land in the fields beyond the town, and a modern asphalt highway winds its way to Santa Fé through high, rocky walls and along an aisle of tall green pines that borders the magnificent gorge of the Rio Grande.

Many automobiles whiz along this highway that once witnessed the tedious march of eastern traders into Santa Fé. The traders traveled for six weeks on wooden wheels, or in the saddle, out from St. Louis, with the heat of the sun, the bone-seeking chill of the night, the scarcity of water and the fear of hostile Indians, eager for loot and scalps, as constant companions. Then, on the horizon, a cluster of adobe houses, the green of trees—Santa Fé.

Now automobiles rise over the last hill and glide easily into town while their riders continue to chatter about whatever interests them. But in the old days the first sight of Santa Fé was hailed with loud whoops of joy that rang out over the wide plateau, with shots from muskets and pistols and the quickened clatter of horses' hoofs as the riders mounted the last hill and swung into town.

In those days, Santa Fé was the home of "good music, good wine and pretty girls." Houses, whitewashed inside and out, were filled with good food, and fine silver and gracious hospitality. They were secluded by high whitewashed walls. Down the narrow, dusty streets men wearing laced trousers, brilliant sashes, great boots of embossed leather, silver spurs, rode horses prancing

27

proudly in lurid trappings. For every man wore his money on his back, and women did the same.

It was said that the girls of Santa Fé were flirtatious but haughty. It is true that they dressed in colors of the rainbow and loaded themselves with barbaric jewelry, that they painted their faces with flour and vermilion and that of many it could be said that they were useful but not respectable.

Among these gala-costumed belles sauntered padres in black cassocks, Spaniards with clinking spurs, traders in fringed buckskin. A colorful pageant moving against the long whitewashed walls that sparkled in the sun.

And at the end of the trail was the tavern—La Fonda. So it is now. But it is a new La Fonda that greets you with heretofore unknown quiet, comfort and crisp cleanliness. Built of adobe in pueblo style, it hugs the earth and seems as if it sprang up at the insistent stamp of an Indian's dancing foot. Within it have been gathered all the popular folk arts of North America. Hooked rugs from Carolina and New England, lacquers from Michoacan, tufted counterpanes from Georgia and Kentucky, tin candelabra and handwrought lanterns from Mexico, paintings from Pueblo Indians, rugs from the Navahos, baskets from the Hopis. Geraniums bloom in countless pots—all different. Birds sing in the patios. Santos give their blessings from the wall niches. Nothing matches; everything harmonizes. That by-the-dozen hostelry look is completely routed. In twenty-four hours you are as devoted to the furnishings of your room or your pet corner of the patio as you are to those around your own fireside.

Indians, tall, quiet, responsive, stalk about the lounge with blankets over their shoulders, black hair framing their brown faces in the austere page-boy cut they prefer, their hands and arms laden with silver and turquoise jewelry. Then the child in you yearns to dress up. Soon your fingers, ears, arms, throat are laden with jewelry, every piece more desirable than another. Proud, gentle, kindly, the vendor waits patiently while you amuse yourself and make your selection. There is no insistence, no urge to buy, no bargaining. There are no reproaches if you make no purchase, but if you do, courteous thanks. The vendor salutes and passes on.

The shops of Santa Fé are as fascinating as those of Paris. To them come all the lovely things made by the Indians of the northern end of the plateau. Blankets and jewelry from the Navahos. Pottery from the nearby pueblos of Santa Clara and San Ildefonso. Baskets and katcina dolls from the Hopis. Weird fetishes from the Zuñis.

These tribes have their homes in a triangle-shaped spread which has its base at Acoma. If you have a map handy, point a pencil at Acoma. Then draw a line northeast, past Santa Fé to Taos, and it will pass through the pueblos of Santa Clara and San Ildefonso. Now draw a line straight westward to the Colorado River. After crossing the Chaco River, it will begin to pass through the land of the Navahos. Now join the point to the Acoma dot, and this last side of the triangle will pass south, through the high mesa where the Hopi lives, down through the sun-drenched home of the Zuñi and thus back to Acoma. Within the limits of this triangle Indian art flourishes today as it did four hundred years ago. Beautiful things are made to sell. They can be yours for very little.

Every pueblo has its art form, its type of decoration, and by some secret reciprocal arrangement they do not overlap. The Keres of Acoma, Laguna and Santa Ana make a crude clay-colored pottery which they sell along the highway for a few cents. North of Santa Fé more finished pottery is made in the pueblos of Santa Clara and San Ildefonso. Taos practices no crafts save a little beadwork on buckskin, which is a craft really borrowed from the white man, since before his coming the Indians did no work with beads. The weaving of blankets and the working of silver are the arts of the Navahos. The Zuñis, who also make silver, have nearly withdrawn from this field in favor of their more industrious and more skilled neighbors, but they make a charming decorated pottery.

The Hopis, who live on flat-topped hills called mesas, are the tailors of the Rio Grande pueblos. They weave sashes and ceremonial garments which they trade for jewelry, blankets and pottery. The Hopis on the first mesa are potters; on the second and third mesas they are basketmakers.

Not only are the various arts themselves confined to certain pueblos, but the sex of those who work in every art is prescribed by custom. The Navaho women weave, the men make jewelry; the Hopi women are the basket-makers and potters, the men the weavers; while in San Ildefonso and Santa Clara the women make the pottery, though occasionally men decorate it.

To know, to understand, to appreciate the things made by their brown hands, it is not enough to see them in shops or in museums. Let us get out into the sun-scorched, water-sculptured Indian country. Meet these brown people who live so intimately with the brown earth. Watch them wrest a meager livelihood from the arid soil, listen to their chants, attend their dances, visit their markets. Only then can we evaluate the popular arts of these plateau primitives.

CHAPTER THREE

Brown Hands and Red Earth

POTTERY, seemingly the most fragile substance made by man, often exists longest. And no printed word ever told more thrilling tales than do the potsherds which litter the Southwestern states and Middle America. They can be read like books, for it has been proved that every people created its own style of pottery. Each locality had its special design. When the people moved, the style changed. And the records of the Indians and of their movements can, with the aid of pottery fragments found in the earth, be traced back as far as two thousand years.

The art of the potter is said to be the second oldest art. First came weaving. It was natural for idle hands to twist a few reeds and a few lengths of grass and make a basket. Gradually the Indians became such expert weavers that their fine baskets would actually hold water. To put hot stones into these baskets and thus to boil food was the second step. Then it was discovered that when earth was plastered about the inside of the coarser baskets, they became waterproof too. One day such a basket got too near the fire, or perhaps the housewife fell asleep at her cooking. While she nodded, the fire burned away the basket, baked the clay, and the first pot was made.

The finest pottery ever yet produced by the plateau peoples was made between A. D. 500 and 1000. When the Spaniards came in the 1500's, the art of making pottery had already declined, but our own century has seen a splendid revival. And today Nampeyo of Hano and Maria Martinez of San Ildefonso have taken their place among the finest ceramic artists of modern times.

Pottery is a noble, an individual art, because it depends upon the maker to a greater degree than does any other craft. There are no recipes for mixing the clay, no methods of testing temperatures, no patterns for guidance. Every step from start to finish depends entirely upon the judgment, the skill and the taste of the maker. Nevertheless, the art does possess tradition.

"Why do you go two miles down the road to get this clay for the slip?" I asked Severa, a potter of Santa Clara, one day. Her quiet brown eyes opened wide in surprise at my question.

33

"We have always gone there," she said. "Our old people taught us that was the place."

And I could not help adding, "Blessed are the ways of the ancients."

The revival of Pueblo pottery really began soon after Dr. Fewkes started to excavate Sakyatli during the last years of the past century. Among the men who worked under him was the husband of Nampeyo, a Hopi woman already known for her fine pottery. When she saw the beautiful designs on the prehistoric pottery dug up at the site of the excavations, she became interested. She began to experiment with different clays and slips. She was most successful, and soon her daughters and other women of her pueblo became interested too. They gave up making the crude cooking pots which the women usually produce—for in the pueblos of the Rio Grande every woman is a potter of sorts. And soon their beautiful wares were in demand.

Much the same thing happened among the Tewa about fifty miles toward the east of Santa Fé, in the villages of San Ildefonso and Santa Clara.

The most beautiful pottery made in San Ildefonso is that of Maria Martinez and her husband Julian and of Susanne Aguila and her husband José. Many years ago, when I first visited this little village on the plateau, Maria had just discovered that she enjoyed making pottery as her grandmother had done, and she had a rare aptitude for it. Tourists and friends who visited there bought Maria's pottery in preference to others'. And in a short time Maria was a celebrity. Her pottery was exhibited in museums and in collections of Indian tribal arts.

Then came the tourists to pester her with questions and compliments. This Maria did not enjoy. She retreated in typical Indian fashion behind a manner aloof, stoical, repellent. I would see her stalking about the streets of San Ildefonso, short, stocky, her brief, full skirt coming halfway between knee and ankle, showing a length of amazingly white buckskin moccasins and legging. A colorful blouse, black hair, cut page-boy fashion, framing her face with metallic smoothness, Navaho rings on those skillful brown hands. Her small black eyes missed nothing. She never smiled. We were afraid to speak to her.

But Maria did take an interest in the young girls of the pueblo. To them she tried to teach this ancient art which had marvelously been reborn in her fingers. The black pottery of San Ildefonso became fashionable. It offered just the right accessory interest for modern interiors. So the little market at San Ildefonso prospered and eclipsed those in other pueblos where the pottery did not meet so ready a welcome with the tourists.

Today, the Hopi women of the first mesa and the Zuñi women also make some pottery. The Keres women are really commercial potters. They turn out cream-colored squat jars decorated with many red and black triangles, with the bird symbols of Cochiti or the bold triangles of Santo Domingo. The cheapest ones sell most quickly, so it is natural that quantity rather than quality has become their goal. At sunup each day the Keres leave their pueblos with their pots to go down to sit by the transcontinental road under the awnings of thatch, ready to approach any car which slows down and whose occupants seem interested or susceptible.

Several types of pottery are produced in the pueblo villages today. Among them are the cooking vessels, which are untempered, without decoration. When they come out of the firing they are a gay orange-red, but this color soon blackens when the pots are exposed to open fires. There is a plain pottery in black and red, or in natural red or sooted black, which has a nice polish, but glaze is as unknown an art today as it was in prehistoric times. The decorated ware is usually black or light, with bottom and interior neck sometimes painted red; a polychrome has black and red designs painted on buff and a dark red ware, black decorations. In Santa Clara and in San Ildefonso is made a shiny black pottery much prized by decorators of modern interiors.

The favorite shapes are those of shallow bowls, trays and low bulbous ollas. There is an interesting vase with a double neck, and there are also ceremonial pieces for holding corn meal during religious rites. These are sometimes rectangular, with steps at one end symbolizing clouds and mountains. The decorations on these pieces are usually fertility symbols, such as frogs, tadpoles and the long snake that carries prayers for rain to the gods underground.

The potters of Acoma make a ware of remarkable

lightness, with charming decorations of parrots and various plant forms. The Zuñi make large low food bowls decorated with animals and squash flower designs—black and red on a warm ivory background. On the first mesa of the Hopi, pottery is made of excellent clays and slips. After firing, its color ranges from a cream to a rich orange, and it is decorated with wide spirals, birds and feathers. None of these pots has the three legs which are characteristic of the pottery of Mexico.

In the pueblo of Santa Clara little animals are made of polished clay fired black. These are really toys for the children, but if you visit the little market frequently, you can get some very charming conceits.

The method of making pottery is much the same in all these Rio Grande pueblos, but since I am most familiar with the work as it is done in San Ildefonso and Santa Clara, I shall tell you about that.

The wheel is never used. It was unknown until the coming of the Spaniards, and to this day the Pueblo potters do not use it, preferring to mold the clay with their own brown hands in the way of the ancients.

These modern potters still go to the old beds to collect white and red clays. They also go to the place their grandmothers went to for the light-gray mineral earth called "temper," which is mixed in the clay to insure toughness and to prevent breakage while it is being fired. They make a slip from a hard yellow stone and black paint from the guaco plant.

When these materials are gathered, work at home begins. First the clays are run through a basket sieve to remove coarse and incorrigible particles. The stone for the slip is pounded up on the metate until it is smooth and fine. The guaco—usually gathered in the spring because it is more tender at that time—is boiled for about six hours until it becomes a sticky black mass. This is put away to age—the longer the better. Finally cow and sheep manure is collected, dried and stacked up along with cedar wood. Now the potter is really ready to start work.

A few broken bits of old pottery are the only molding tray she needs. These help her to revolve the pot and thus bring every surface in contact with her hand. She has a few gourd spoons of different sizes, a knife of tin or steel which she uses to shape and smooth the pieces, and an old sack or a goatskin is quite satisfactory to mix the clay in. A Standard Oil can or pail filled with water always stands near, to be used when the clay needs softening.

Brushes for applying the design are nothing more than slivers from the yucca, chewed and trimmed. Rags are used to brush on the slip, and any old board is all right to hold the pot while it is drying. The two little polishing pebbles—one larger than the other—are the most prized possessions of the potter.

These are often heirlooms. Some have a sacred significance, and when Severa promised to let me use her polishing stones if I would remain at Santa Clara and make pottery with her, I was too deeply touched to do more than hold her slender hands in mine. She understood my silence and my thoughts.

With her tools and brushes and clay about her, the potter squats down on the warm earth to work in the shade. First she takes a lump of clay and pats and presses it into a round, flat mass like a pancake. Then small pieces of clay are rubbed between the palms, or between palm and earth, until they become elongated into round, narrow coils. With the "pancake" as a base, the potter builds these coils up the sides until the vessel takes on the height and shape she has in mind. Meanwhile the clay is moistened to keep it pliable. With fingers and spoons, perhaps with a knife, she smooths the vessel inside and out until the ridges of the coils disappear. Then the polishing begins. The small pebble is used inside, the larger one outside. For hours and hours the skilled brown hands pass the smooth pebble over and over the pot, and when it answers to her wish, she sets it aside to dry in the sun before firing. If the vessel is to be decorated, it is given a slip of clay. Slip is ground yellow stone diluted with water until it is almost liquid. Then the design is applied.

When you watch the potters at work, you come to await one certain moment, just as you do when you watch airplanes about to land or listen to a musician approach a difficult cadenza. It is the moment when the pot is ready for its decoration.

Some take up the pot, hold it a moment in their hands, looking at it with intense concentration. Then they seize the brushes and start to paint. Others take up the pot, look out at the sun, the clouds, the sky, as if their minds were far away, then suddenly start to cover it with quick, firm lines. And there are other potters who never pause. There may be six, ten, fifteen pots before them (they seldom work on only one at a time), but the complete plan for each one's decoration seems already to be full-fledged in their brain. Once applied, the decoration can never be altered.

The designs used on pottery are said to have the same source as has the art itself—weaving. The same symbols of clouds, lightning, falling rain appear frequently. However, animal and plant designs are also used.

Any smooth, dry, level spot protected from the wind is good enough for the kiln; yet firing is the most delicate part of the work. Hours of careful molding, polishing, decorating can end in zero if the firing is not right. The kilns are made of old stove grates or just iron junk supported on tin cans. The pieces are put in upside down, quite close together. Around the grate a wall is built of dried dung, from which the pots are protected with stones and bricks. Cedar is used to start the fire, which is fed with manure. Firing is started on all sides at once so that the heat may be even. It requires about half an hour, and during this time air must be kept circulating through the crude kiln. White slips come from the firing a pinkish brown; red appears darker, and yellow changes to a rich orange-red.

When the pots are to be black, the firing is done as

described previously, but just before they are removed, the pots are covered with manure. This causes the smoke to remain within the kiln, and the carbon from the smoke becomes ingrained in the pottery. The result is a stunning soot-black color.

There are little pottery shops in San Ildefonso, and some of the adobe huts that cluster beneath the shadow of the high black mesa that vaults up into the air and gives the town its name, "Sacred Island of Defense," now have signs announcing the names of the potters and artists who live in them. I love to buy in Santa Clara, for that little village, whose Indian name means "where the wild rosebushes grow near the water," has the most charming open-air market in the Southwest.

The usual approach to the village is along a dusty, sunny road that leaves Santa Fé to wind northwest along the plateau, occasionally glimpsing the shining waters of the Rio Grande. This is historic territory, and the landscape echoes the tumult of the past. It is a wrath of color —red, yellow, brown clay; blue sage, green cactus, flaming red ocatillo. Over all, a sky of such intense blue that it hurts your eyes, a yellow sun as penetrating as an X-ray. You spin past arroyos that are but channels of rocks, strewn as if by the hand of an angry and relentless god. Occasionally you see brown men in blue jeans working in the irrigation ditches. The ancestors of these people were the first to irrigate these arid lands and make them fertile. They began this practice as long ago as the fourteenth century, when the Tewa were a powerful and numerous people inhabiting all the land now bordered by Colorado on the north and Texas on the south.

When the Spaniards came marching north, these people had no less than fifty villages on the banks of the great river. As early as 1640 more than six thousand were baptized by the padres. Now there are but six villages with a population of a mere thousand.

Today this decimated tribe is divided into two groups —the winter and the summer people. Each one has its leaders, who serve for life, but only during six months of each year. They go to mass in the morning, for the people of this tribe were among the first to accept Catholicism. What else could they do? Their villages did not know the protection of the Hopi's high mesa. Exposed to attack, they were forced to greet the whites with smiles and to cling to their old ways secretly. After mass the Tewa return home to dress in their ceremonial clothes and to reappear on the plaza and take part in the corn dance in summer, the deer and buffalo dances during the hunting season. Thus they address their own gods in the ways of the ancients.

After a half hour's motoring from Santa Fé, you see mounds of earth piercing the horizon. Soon these take form as large cubes, and then you recognize a village of small adobe huts set down on the sunny plain. As your car approaches, you hear nothing, but you see tiny black-clad figures running between the houses. By the time your car stops in the dusty plaza all the hurrying and the excitement you have witnessed from afar are ended.

Standing in the center of the plaza is a semicircle of small figures completely enveloped in long black shawls that cover their heads and fall to their ankles. At the feet of each figure black and red pots are arranged on the earth in neat groups. There is no sound. No one speaks, and you yourself seem strangely silenced before this gentle dignity.

You start to make the rounds of the circle. You pick up this pot and that—this little toy and then still another. You ask a price. The reply is given in a voice as soft and low as a flute. You walk around the circle inspecting the wares. If you look back to survey a pot or to compare one passed by with one before you, the vendor may step forward, but not unless you invite her. Yet there is nothing servile in the attitude of these picturesque saleswomen. They have a gracious dignity, a courtesy, silent yet eloquent, that proclaims them aristocrats more emphatically than crests and coats of arms could ever do.

In such surroundings it is a pity to make purchases with money. You find yourself longing for the more romantic exchange of earlier days—for parrot feathers, shells, coral, turquoise, even beads. Perhaps my mind was preoccupied with this idea when I gave a little girl two dollars instead of one in payment for a lovely black bowl. I did not notice my error, and after visiting some friends who live in the pueblo, I got into my car to go home. As the car whirled down the road, something made me look back. A little black-shawled figure was running behind us. I watched for a moment. A cloud of dust swirled around the runner, but she kept on. Something was wrong. We stopped. In a few moments the little runner came panting up to the car. She waved a dollar bill frantically and sank down on the fender. Finally, between gasps, she made me understand that the dollar was mine. I had to take it; to do otherwise would have been discourteous. Yet that dollar meant so little to me, so much to the child. I helped her into the car and started back to the village. A few paces down the road, I glanced into the little brown face closely framed in the black calico shawl. The smile on the child's face was beatific. Then the reason came to me—she was riding in an automobile!

When the car drove through the village, from every house door, from behind every shed a child's face peered. We stopped before her mother's door, and she thanked me with the grace of a queen for returning her child.

When selecting pottery, take a tip from the Indian. Flick it with your first finger snapped against your thumb. If the ring is clear you will know that there is no weak flaw in the clay. The pot is strong and should last you well.

Then observe the pot for shape. I have illustrated on page 199 several fine forms that are characteristic of pueblo pottery. These shapes have been made by the Indian for centuries, and you will at once notice their grace, the beauty of their proportions and the fact that they sit down well. The posture of a pot is as important to beauty as good posture is in a woman. A carelessly made pot will lean to one side or be unsteady or look uneven. Always place a pot on an even surface, then step back and look at it before you finally decide to buy it.

Luster must also be considered. The Indians never mastered the art of glazing—that is, the use of metallic washes to enhance the gloss and strengthen the wares— but they use a polishing stone and thus bring up a very high luster. The better pots are almost mirror-like in their sheen. This gloss extends evenly all over their surface and is one invariable characteristic of fine pottery.

After testing the ring, observing the shape and luster, you must consider the color and design. The coloring should be even in intensity. The design should be drawn on clearly, with lines even and well-defined. The cheap, tawdry pot will be noticeable for a careless, slovenly drawn design. On the better piece the design will seem to belong to the pot. It will appear to have been "born" with it. This is difficult to describe but easy to recognize. If the design seems large, unevenly spaced or overbold, look for another pot. But if the design seems to flow gracefully around the pot, with interesting variations, you know that it has been applied by a master. Buy it and cherish it.

You will notice that I have not mentioned size. I consider it of minor importance. It takes great skill to mold large bowls, vases and jugs, but their showiness must yield before a small piece that rings clearly, that is symmetrically shaped, evenly colored, lustrous and distinctively designed. Do not let size distract you. Demand of every piece these requisite qualities and you will have pottery that museums will someday want.

Decorators of modern interiors have seized eagerly upon the dramatic black and the orange-red pottery of the pueblos to use as accessories in every room in the house. The simple functional shapes, the strong color and dull luster are ideally suited to such a style of decoration. In modern rooms the low bowls and bulbous vases are effective aids to striking flower arrangements, particularly when brilliant dahlias, zinnias, asters are chosen for the bouquet. White calla lilies clustered in these black vases make a thrilling effect in a room done in the popular white leathers and white homespuns so often used in contemporary interiors. If the bouquet is misted with baby's breath, it is equally beautiful in a more florid setting.

Shallow, low black bowls placed on tables of bleached woods and filled with pebbles which hold erect jonquils, daffodils, narcissuses or irises make stunning table centerpieces. For the short-stemmed flowers—violets, pansies, marigolds, bachelor's-buttons—the smaller black bowls made at both Santa Clara and San Ildefonso provide the ideal and infrequently found vase.

A flat, plate-shaped dish is now being made in these pueblos. It is undecorated save for a simple motif of the same color but of higher gloss. If you can secure enough of these plates to be combined with one of the large shallow bowls and thus make up a salad set, you are fortunate. Arrange them on a corn-colored cloth and serve a tossed-up green salad. On the hottest summer day such an ensemble will give you an appetite.

Equally harmonious with peasant and provincial interiors are the beautiful bowls made by the Hopis on the first mesa. Their soft yellow-reds and cream clays, decorated in designs that are similar to those of the ancients, mate effectively with the colors in rooms furnished in maple, fruit wood and pine. Yet they are seldom seen.

Fill one of these low wide bowls with oranges, apples, nuts, peppers, raisins, eggplant for a Thanksgiving Day table centerpiece, and you cannot have a richer, more festive decoration. Use them on porches, window sills, and garden steps to hold pots of geraniums and other gay-colored flowering plants, and you'll find real enjoyment in the new vogue of flowerpot gardening.

But let me give you this one suggestion—it is wise to shellac the inside of all pueblo pottery before you use it. It is made to store corn and beans and therefore is not waterproof, but a very few cents' worth of shellac and five minutes' time will remedy this deficiency and allow these decorative wares to lend interest and charm to your home—delightful reminders of your days in Indian country.

CHAPTER FOUR

Basketry of the Far Mesas

THE isolation of the Hopis has been ended by the automobile. For at least four hundred years they lived secluded on their high mesas. Even the Spaniards, whose will to conquer transcends all credibility, left them to themselves, and when the marauding Navaho and acquisitive white man came, they seldom molested them. The name *Hopikuh* means "Peaceful Ones," and they have lived true to their name for the very practical reason that it was difficult to attack them and they therefore had no cause to fight.

The Hopis live on three mesas more than a hundred miles north of Flagstaff, Arizona. These flat-topped hills skyrocket up from the valley floor to a great height. But this rocky pedestal is not barren. Springs bubble up from its depths and provide the most cherished of all things on this arid plateau—water. The first mesa, Shungapai, "Spring Where Narrow Reeds Grow," can be reached by car from the transcontinental railroad in half a day.

At first you speed over a flat, dusty plain, but it is not long before the ascent begins. Soon you can look over the sides of the pass at fertile fields below, on which play the shadows of cumulus clouds. The high corn waves in the breeze, and patches of green mosaic the plain. You ride on, and soon the road curves seem to end in sky. On the second mesa is Walpi, "Place of the Gap," famous as the site of the autumnal snake dance, and on the third mesa is the oldest modern city of this ancient plateau civilization, now nearly deserted—Oraibi.

At the tops of the narrow mesas sandstone houses are clustered in terraces that rise as high as three stories. They hug the rock so closely that they seem to be a part of it. The first floor of these houses is usually used as a storeroom for corn, beans, watermelons, pumpkins. The second floor is the living room and is reached by a ladder. This room is invariably neat and clean; oftentimes the walls are tinted, niches contain cooking vessels, sometimes katcinas, and there are many pegs on which clothes are neatly hung. Families bask on the roof in the sunshine, and never were there more adorable children than those of the Hopis. They are always smiling.

The Hopis are a happy people, even when the whites are around. Their manner is gentle, gracious, almost suave. They are alert, well poised, but around them hovers a peculiar acrid smell, offensive to the white nose at first meeting. Perhaps their most amazing characteristic is their attitude toward the snake. These mysterious creatures that live beneath the earth are believed to be messengers of the gods, for Pueblo gods live underground. Therefore, the Hopi reveres the snake, loves him as a brother and performs his rituals with his aid, but no Hopi ever seems to suffer from snake bite—a mystery that is still unsolved.

The men of the Hopi tribe are industrious. As you approach their mesa, you come upon their corn and pumpkin fields as far off as fifteen miles. The men are farmers in summer and in winter, weavers; the women make baskets, except on the first mesa, where pottery is the craft of the tribe. These baskets are made not only for sale but also for use, because the basket still plays an important part in Hopi ceremonials. Theirs is a most intensive ritual. Every day, occasion, season has its special ceremony, which is often long. Nine days is the usual term of preparation for the ceremony itself, which may last for seven more days, although in the summer shorter ceremonies and dances are held.

Trays are the chief form which Hopi ceremonial baskets take. They are used to carry the sacred corn meal in many rituals. During the marriage ceremony, the bride carries a tray of corn meal to her in-laws to "pay for her husband." Trays are used to serve food at all important feasts; to offer food to one's ancestors; to carry prayer-sticks; and the legend says that it is on a tray that one's spirit at death is carried over the river of the Grand Canyon to the Hopi heaven.

Basketry is also used by the Hopi for cooking utensils, for sieves, water bottles, bowls. It shades the sunny doorways, hoods the fireplace and cradles the baby. It is their china, leather, glass, metal. Now the sale of baskets to tourists has become an important source of income as well.

Countless legends tell the story of the Hopi's discovery of basketry and of different kinds of baskets. One of the chief legends is about Tiyo, their mythical snake hero.

Tiyo and his father lived near the junction of the San Juan and the Colorado rivers. The boy, who was thoughtful and studious, wondered about the constant flowing away of the waters of the Colorado. He decided to try to solve the mystery.

His father helped him hew a closed canoe out of a cottonwood tree so that he might make the trip secretly. His mother and sister gave him a po-o-to, a basket tray made of yucca, heaped it with food, and he started out on his dangerous trip.

When he reached the end of his journey, he saw a small hole in the ground, and as he walked toward it, a voice greeted him. "Up-*pi*-tuh, my heart is glad! I have long been expecting you. Come down into my house."

Tiyo did so, and led by the Spider Woman—for it was she who had greeted him—he visited the underworld and learned all the songs, prayers, dances and ceremonials

51

that are now performed by the Snake-Antelope frater-nity of the Hopi tribe.

Tiyo and the Spider Woman visited the Sun and learned many things. When they returned to the Kiva, the chief gave him two maidens. He said, "Here are two maidens who know the charm which prevents death from the bite of a rattlesnake. Take them with you, and one give to your younger brother."

Four days later the Spider Woman (the mythical weaver of clouds) made a beautiful basket fastened with a cotton cord. She told Tiyo and the maidens to get in it. Then she disappeared down a hatch. Soon a filament descended, attached itself to the cord, and the basket was drawn up to the clouds.

In this way the Spider Woman returned Tiyo and the two maidens to his mother's house, and the first basket came to earth.

The descendants of Tiyo and his brother and the two maidens who became their wives are today members of the Snake and of the Antelope clans which perform the thrilling plea for rain in which baskets filled with sacred corn meal and rattlesnakes play an important part.

The Navahos, who seldom make baskets, though they use them in their rituals and as cradles for their babies, tell a beautiful legend of the making of the first cradle basket.

The gods of war were born of two women. One was fathered by the Sun, and the other by the Waterfall.

When they were born, they were placed in baby baskets made alike. The footrests and the back battens were made of sunbeams; the heads, of rainbow; the sides were strings of sheet lightning and the lacing, strings of zig-zag lightning. One child was covered with the black cloud and the other with the female rain.

But the legend of the real beginning of basketry comes from the Yakima Indians. They say that once the world was all water, and the Saghalu Tyce was above it. He threw up out of the water at the shallow places great quantities of mud. Thus land was made. He made trees grow. He made man out of a ball of mud and told him what to do. When man grew lonely, he made woman. He taught her to dress, to spin, to gather berries, to find barks of roots from which to make baskets.

One day while she was sleeping, she dreamed of her ignorance of how to please man, and then she prayed Saghalu Tyce to aid her. He heard her prayer, breathed on her and, in so doing, gave her something to help her which could not be seen, heard, smelled, or touched. It was kept in a tiny basket, and by it all the arts of design and handiwork were given to the hands of the descend-ants of woman.

There are hundreds of fanciful legends about basketry and its origin, but the fact is that basketmaking undoubt-edly began with the weaving of nets. In early days gourds were used to carry water. They were clumsy to handle, difficult to transport and fragile. Undoubtedly an inven-tive woman devised the idea of a net to strengthen the gourd and to permit easier carrying. Years ago a good weaver of baskets was prized as a wife. A man might even pay as much as two strings of shell—one hundred dollars—for her if she were expert. Today basketry is an industry common to all Indian women, just as pottery is, but it is an art that is rapidly declining.

The Hopi makes baskets of two materials, the willow and the yucca. Willow baskets are made in Oraibi, but all five villages of the middle mesa make the yucca tray. These are built upon a coil made of a thick bundle of the woody yucca stems and sewn together with a thread made of the split leaf of this same tree.

This craft requires an intimate knowledge of wood, fiber and grass as well as manual skill. One must know, not only what to use, but where and when and how to collect the necessary materials. The Indian woman's discovery of the willow, the yucca and the maidenhair fern as well as of the herbs which give them glowing color, must have been by a trial-and-error procedure, requiring countless years and endless effort. But tradition has carried down through the years, and now these people are adept at the craft.

Willows are gathered at the time they are most pliable. Sumac and fern are cut when they split best. The yucca is cut from the mature plant when a yellow-green color is desired. If a bright green is wanted, only fresh shoots are used, while the heart leaves provide white fibers.

Long ago basketmakers used an awl or stiletto of bone or a stone knife, but now scissors, teeth, and nails suffice as tools. The material used for sewing the coils is willow twig from which the bark has been removed. The twig is then split and trimmed to a convenient size.

When baskets are made for sale, aniline dyes are largely used; but when baskets are made for use, the old vegetable dyes are still brewed with great labor and patience. Devil's claw gives a black dye; the maidenhair fern provides a deep brown; yucca roots give a rich red. When the squaw grass is soaked in water, it turns yellow; when soaked in very hot water, a deep brown results. The mordant (the substance used to fix the color) preferred is the same as that so frequently used when dyeing wool —urine.

The colors have a sacred significance which varies with the tribes. Among the Hopi the sacred colors of the cardinal points are yellow, green, red and white. Among the Zuñi the north is designated as yellow, the west is blue, the south is red and the east is white, the upper region (the Pueblos have six cardinal points, up and down being considered points as well as north, south, east and west) is many-colored and the lower region, black. The Navahos explain their colors differently. "The eagle plumes are laid to the *east* and nearby them the *white* corn and white shell; the *blue* feathers were laid to the *south* with blue corn and turquoise; the hawk feathers were laid to the *west* with *yellow* corn and abalone shell; and to the *north* were laid the whippoorwill feathers with black beads and corn of all colors." Thus we have the

Navaho color chart reading: east, white; south, blue; west, yellow; and north, black.

When making the trays, the Hopis begin with a flat coil. This type of basket is difficult and tedious to start. Often a group of women will get together for a basket bee and start a large number of these coils. Gossip and companionship help them to forget the tedious task their fingers pursue.

The baskets usually take the forms of trays or plaques. Cone-shaped carrying baskets, baby cradles, carrying mats and baskets to be used as water bottles are now seldom seen, and boiling baskets are almost never used. Sometimes the carrying ring may still be seen. This is a ring plaited of yucca which aids the woman when balancing a round-bottomed basket or bowl on her head. Coronado was so intrigued with this gadget that he sent two to the Viceroy of Mexico with this message:

I send your worship two rolles, which the women in these parts are wont to wear on their heads when they fetch water from their wells, as we used to do in Spain, and one of these Indian women with one of these rolles on her head will carry a pitcher of water, without touching the same, up a lather [ladder].

Pueblo basketry designs can be divided into four groups: animal designs—eagles, butterflies, birds, cleverly stylized to conform to the limitations of the medium; vegetable designs, such as flowers, leaves, trees, ferns;

natural designs, such as rain, clouds, lightning, inter-
preted with horizontal and zigzag lines; artificial designs,
such as arrows and crosses. Occasionally the fantastic figure of a katcina is woven into the Hopi plaques.

In addition to the weaving in of designs, the baskets
are ornamented in several ways: by a combination of
weaves done in one color; by a simple weave worked in
with several colors; by a combination of weaves in a single color or a combination of colors; and by adding feathers, fur or shells. This latter type of ornamentation is
seldom used among the Pueblo peoples.

Whether or not the designs are symbolic is a much
debated question. Certainly many of the most frequently
used designs have names with wide acceptance, but it is
generally believed among those who have known the Indian intimately that the designs are not symbolic but imi-
tative and imaginative.

Living high on the plateau intimately with nature,
whose phenomona decreed the life or death of the tribes,
it was natural that the Indian should be deeply conscious
of the forks of lightning, the terrace of the clouds, the rise
and fall of the mountains, the arch of the rainbow, the
spiral of flying birds, the stars and sun. And in like manner, the animals that were associated with rain and food
became important. How natural then to weave these designs into the utensils used in daily life!

To question the Indian woman about her designs is seldom the way to get an answer that holds even a degree of
truth. She will resent your curiosity and answer "yes" or

"no" as she thinks you wish to be answered, or she will gaily laugh away the questions. One who made friends with an Indian did win from her this tragic explanation of her basket plaque:

> The coils of my basket are like the people of my race. They begin in a wide sweep, but grow smaller and smaller until they end in a dot. So my people, who once swarmed over this plateau, are fading away. Soon we will disappear, as does the dot of my basket.

There is one custom that is symbolic and is always recognized by the Hopi. This is the "finishing off" of their yucca plaques. When a marriageable virgin is making the tray, the inner grass is allowed to "flow out." This is termed the "flowing gate." To close it would be to render the weaver incapable of bearing children and therefore confine her to a life of loneliness and sorrow. Widows and married women "taper down" this inner coil when finishing their trays, and this tapered coil is termed the "closed gate." Blessed with children, the matron may make the ends of the grass shorter, while with the widow there is no hope of maternity, and she may therefore close the gate.

In all ceremonials in which baskets are used, the position in which the closing point is held is deemed important, and those who know the Indian say that there is still much investigation to be done on the matter of the symbolic form of the baskets.

There is something very personal and appealing about Indian baskets. No two are ever alike in color or design. The wonder of their making never loses its fascination. Before this bit of color and design came into being, every piece of material had to be carefully selected. This required hours and maybe days of testing and searching among trees and bushes under the scorching sun of the plateau. Then brown hands had to weave the grasses and fibers and twigs carefully together, smoothly, with perfectly even spaces. The line must be kept strong, clear, well-defined. The proportions must be right, not only in size and shape but also in design. The beauty of the color harmonies, the rhythm of the line of the design, these the basket weaver must keep constantly in mind, for there are no patterns to guide her. And brown hands must be so obedient, so skillful that mind and fingers work as one to produce perfection.

There are several important rules to consider when selecting baskets for a collection. They must be studied for perfection of weave and symmetry of outline. The delicacy of the thread and evenness of stitch are important as well as the choice of materials, pattern and ornamentation. The size is least important of all, for it does not govern beauty nor quality.

Last and most important is the general effect which is produced by all these factors and the appeal of the basket to *you*. Do not begrudge the hours you spend studying baskets before you finally decide to buy in the shops or directly from the Indians. The inventive genius, the fertility of resource, the incredible patience of the Indian woman, who, with her rare taste for fitness and beauty, and her amazingly dexterous hands, weaves so wonderfully, will not fail to thrill you at first sight and to fascinate you more and more as you study the products of her unique genius.

The basket plays an important role in nearly all Indian rituals of the Pueblo tribes. In September and October, the Hopis dance the Lagon—the woman's Basket Dance. This is given by the Lalakonti Society in even-numbered years in five Hopi villages and is inaugurated with the usual preparation of all important Hopi rituals —rites in the Kiva such as sand paintings, initiations, bajo-making, chantings, messengers. On the ninth day there is a race at dawn. A beautifully dressed Hopi girl bearing a sacred basket stands while women and girls race up the trail to the waiting circle of priestesses who have assembled in the plaza.

The dance begins in the afternoon. The priestesses again gather in the plaza, bearing baskets and chanting. The baskets are held in both hands with the concave side to the front. In time with the chant, the dancers raise their baskets from below the hips, first to one breast, then to the other, and again lower them to the hips.

Then two girls, elaborately dressed, with bundles on their backs, appear in the circle, untie the bundles, take out baskets, hold them above their heads and exchange places back and forth. Suddenly they throw the baskets high into the air. The young men who have been watching at the edge of the crowd now dash up and struggle to get the prize baskets. This basket dance, like so many Hopi ceremonials, is a dance of fertility and harvest and is accompanied not only by solemn chanting but also by some crude fun making.

The white people have been welcomed to the Hopi dances for more than thirty years. So far the presence of foreign spectators has not made the dancers self-conscious, but the danger exists nevertheless. When his beliefs, rituals and ceremonial customs are approached with courteous curiosity, the Indian is never resentful. More often he is kindly and helpful. But let ridicule, loud laughter, smart-aleck questioning occur, he freezes and sometimes strikes back with a cruel and cutting wit.

These ceremonials of the Hopi and other Pueblo tribes are the most colorful pageants that exist in the world today, certainly the most colorful in America. The costumes woven and embroidered by the men are extremely beautiful. Masks are worn in the winter ceremonials to intensify the idea of the presence of supernatural beings and mythological animals. The colorings of these masks are magnificent. The designs carved and painted on them are always symbolic, and as art, they are masterpieces of design, color and drama. Yet they are made of the simplest materials in the crudest way. Only leather, cloth, feathers, branches are used to make them.

Hopi ceremonies may be divided into two groups. In the first are the elaborate ones which require nine days of preparation and really last sixteen days and which have long, solemn rituals. These take place usually in the fall and winter months when time can be spared from the farms. Then during the spring and summer months shorter rituals take place, beginning with the coming of the katcinas in early spring and ending with the social dances in the early fall. If you are planning a trip to this southwestern plateau, by all means time it so that you may witness at least one ceremonial. To assist you in making your plans, I am writing on pages 216–217 a calendar of Pueblo ceremonials. But now let me tell you about the beautiful katcinas made by these fanciful people.

The katcina is a Pueblo conception. Katcinas are not gods but the spirit or manifestation of the gods who personify clouds, sky, storms, plants, stones, mountains. There are hundreds of Hopi katcinas. Many have passed beyond the memory of moderns, and new ones are always being added to their pantheon. The Hopi personalizes everything, organic and inorganic, and believes that all these spirits can exert a power for good or for evil but that they will yield to the will of humans if they are rightly propitiated. The Hopi also believes that the breath-body, or spirit, continues to exist after death. The katcina is the spirit or personified power of the ancients or other personified object. The Zuñis and Keres also have katcinas, and many Hopi representations have names borrowed from the language of these tribes.

These all-powerful beings can be reached by appeals to the katcinas who come into the Hopi villages from November to January and through the spring and who go out with the Niman katcina in July.

The katcina may be in reality a man who dances in a mask carved of cottonwood or made of basketry, painted and feathered; or it may be a doll, also carved of cottonwood and decorated with paint, cloth and feathers. During the spring and summer these katcina dolls are seen everywhere. Men carve and paint them and set them up in niches in the walls of their homes, and the children play with them as dolls. Dr. Fewkes, who lived for many years among the Hopis, studying their ceremonies, collected in 1880 more than two hundred pictures of katcinas drawn by Hopi artists.

When the Hopi makes a mask to be worn by a man who will represent the katcina or makes a doll also representing the katcina, he decorates it with symbols that are characteristic of the spirit of the being who is to be impersonated. The head is out of all proportion to the size of the body, and great care is taken in carving and painting it.

The decorations of these masks or dolls are the rain terraces, squash blossoms, sprouting seeds, the curved rainbow symbol or the zigzag line representing lightning, all of which are indicative of rain and therefore of fertility. The colors used are usually green, black, yellow, white, red, and when the katcinas are painted, the flat colors are usually sprayed from the mouth.

Some of these katcinas are terrifying. They have strangely elongated or bulging globular eyes, protruding snouts, eagle-shaped beaks, great swollen lips, huge red tongues and enormous white teeth.

The symbols painted on the katcina masks and dolls instantly tell the Hopi who he or she is, and every katcina has a name. But it can never be spoken aloud.

The masks are finished with ruffs of fur, spruce, pine or feathers. The dolls and men have their bodies daubed with colored paint or wear ceremonial kilts, shirts, sashes and blankets. They carry eagle, turkey or parrot feathers or bean sprouts, ears of corn, skin pouches filled with sacred corn meal, gourd bottles filled with water from the sacred springs and perhaps yucca whips. The women, katcinamammas, are always impersonated by men and wear long wigs with the hair arranged in a swirl over each ear, thus typifying the squash blossom. This was the manner of hairdressing followed by all marriageable Hopi girls until they learned at the government school to cut their hair into prosaic bobs.

One group is known as the Mudheads. They are the clowns. Their bodies are daubed with clay, and they wear sacks over their heads. They are the fun makers who hoot, yelp, prance about the plaza and have complete license in all their fun making.

The Hopis do not know the Roman calendar. Their year is divided into two seasons—winter and summer. Winter runs approximately from our August to March, and summer extends through the remaining months. The katcinas sometimes come in November, but usually at the beginning of bean-sprouting time, about the middle of

January, although the ceremonies vary from year to year. They "go out" in July, at the close of the Niman festival, one of the most important ceremonials of the Hopi calendar.

Every fourth year the ceremony of the initiation of the children is held. Then the flogging katcinas—Tunwupkatcina—enter the villages from the west and with strange movements and horrifying, hooting cries dance to the plaza. They are terrifying beings with great bulging eyes, horns, big red tongues lolling from mouths filled with enormous teeth. They carry yucca whips and snap them as they prance about.

Then boys and girls are stripped of their clothes by their parents and led up to the monsters. Every little bare brown back receives five or six lashes from the yucca whips, although if the child seems unduly terrified, the whip often misses its mark. The children scream and cry, and the louder their protestation, the better the "medicine" is thought to be. Even grown-ups sometimes fling themselves before the katcinas and receive a thorough trouncing, which is believed to possess curative powers.

This whipping of the children is said to reveal to them the secret of life. Afterwards there are secret dances in the kiva, where the katcinas remove their masks and give their whips to the children, who then whip them. But no child ever tells an uninitiated one who the katcinas are.

As an art form the katcina dolls and masks are one of the most fantastic and colorful known to this hemisphere. They possess all the attributes of beauty characteristic of primitive art: grotesque emphasis to secure a desired effect, decorations in clear primary colors, with every line and every kind of trimming deeply traditional. The emotions they are intended to arouse are obvious at first sight. There are smug complacency, beneficence, gluttony, obscenity, austerity, hauteur, terror and a gay, jolly humor that sends you into gales of laughter. All through the year, from November to July, if you visit the Indian country you may see these interesting impersonations on the altars in the Hopi homes and cuddled lovingly in the hands of their children at play.

Recently the government schools have given paint, brush and paper to the Indian boys and girls, and a new and wonderful art has come to the plateau. These children, whose tastes have never been contaminated with sophisticated ideas of art, are painting pictures with the same crisp line and jewellike color that make the art of the ancient Persians the admiration of modern connoisseurs.

Pueblo children paint what they know—the ceremonial dances of their tribes; animals, horses, buffalo, deer, antelope; and one of their favorite subjects is katcinas.

In the composition of their paintings there is a complete absence of background and absolute freedom from the accepted sense of perspective; yet it is well ordered and balanced. The excellent color rhythm in the delineation of the figures is decorative and disciplined. The result is a flat, decorative mural type of painting, strangely touched with reverence and artistry.

Already several collectors of art have purchased these paintings for their galleries. Their price is easily within the range of all budgets, even the most modest. They possess all the beauty of the primitive without the price-premium that invariably accompanies the antique.

CHAPTER FIVE

The Navaho Blanket and Its Weaver

WHEN you get to Navaholand, you wonder where the Navahos are. You see no clusters of huts, no adobe terraces with sociable ladders mounting from roof to roof; only barren desert stretching toward a distant horizon bound by a necklace of purple mountains. As far as your eye can see there is only earth, sagebrush, mountain, sky —brown, green, purple, blue.

The air is crisp, tangy, for you are on a plateau near the Colorado River, with an elevation of about four thousand feet, and cool breezes blow down from the mountains that tower up to heights of nine and ten thousand feet. Here the nights are cold, the days hot, with a sun that knows no shade. The scene is bare, desolate.

But there is beauty here, the same beauty one glimpses at sea—the beauty of far vistas and of cloudless sapphire skies. The very emptiness of the landscape challenges your imagination, and as you ride along with only your horse for company, you come to understand the poetic yearnings of the Navaho that are so appealingly expressed in their names of places: "Where Water Flows in Darkness under Rocks," "Scattered Springs," "Beautiful in the Mountains," "Where Cranes Stand," or "The Buttes That Stand Like Seven Stars."

No one can visit this country without responding to its bare beauty, without becoming aware of the primitive forces of nature and without longing to throw off the shackles of a mechanized and sophisticated civilization. When this mood comes, you begin to understand one element of the Indian character, his worship of nature, his obedience to habit, his trust in the wisdom of the ways of the ancients.

The Navaho believes that he belongs to this earth. Deeply, silently this idea possesses him and governs his thoughts and customs. That is why he is able to keep contact with great illusions, why with twigs and herbs, with the earth and its metals, the wool of sheep that graze on its pastures, his brown hands make things of rare beauty which are in truth the evidence of the poetic urge which earth, sky, water, and the forces of nature breed deep within him. You feel that same urge when you come to Navaholand.

You ride on. Suddenly in the shade of a cottonwood

69

you see a woman sitting on the ground weaving. Looking beyond the squatting figure, you gradually discern her home. The Navaho hogan is nothing more than a few branches standing upright before the wall of an arroyo or a rock. It is covered with thatch and bark and earth, with an open door facing the east. To you it seems a crude shelter, but to the Navaho there is beauty in the strength of the timbers, the smoothness of the earth floor, the good bark roof that permits the piling on of the protective earth-covering and the dryness and the warmth that linger within.

It is said by old Navahos that these crude hogans are really an improvement over their long-accustomed homes, that the Navahos formerly lived in dugouts, with only a covering of yucca mat, tied down with yucca cords. A ladder descended into the home and was pulled in after it was used. Then, when the family wished to move on, the only work to be done was to fold the yucca mat around the ladder, tie the two together for easy carrying, and pass on.

Today, the hogan is built by the Navaho and his friends with much ceremony. It requires several days for the ritual, in which the wife also takes part. Navaho chants are sung, and finally a feast is placed before the guests, after which they return to their own hogans. For the Navaho cherishes his loneliness. He wants only his own about him. For company, he goes to the trading post and to the long sings and dance ceremonials which take place with great frequency during the winter months. Between times, the Navaho buys, sells, trades horses, makes jewelry of silver, turquoise and coral, and the squaw and children see to the sheep and the weaving.

The Navahos have clung to their customs and beliefs more closely than almost any other of the tribes. Their dress, food, homes, religion, language, habits and opinions have remained unchanged for centuries. They have taken what they wanted from other cultures with nonchalant arrogance. For they consider themselves aristocrats, even calling themselves *diin,* meaning "the people." Legends and ethnologists say the Navahos came down from the north some thousand years ago and that they immediately proceeded to usurp lands, women, crops, sheep, weaving.

A proof of this theory is the fact that, unlike most of the other tribes, the Navahos have no tribal resemblance. Among them you find the tall and the short, the slim and the fat, and you may even see a few gray-eyed men and women. They are a compound of all Indian stocks of this plateau, with a little Spanish blood and perhaps that of Jewish traders thrown in for good measure. The result is a silent, aloof, imaginative, intelligent and proud people capable of a strong, almost cruel humor. Their dress is picturesque—gay-hued velvetine shirts and blouses, full skirts, quantities of turquoise, coral and silver jewelry on neck, wrist and hand. They are amused by the white man rather than respectful toward him, calling white people, with typical caustic wit, *gaa,* meaning "rabbit", because they jump and run so much.

It was the famous Kit Carson who finally brought the Navahos to acknowledge the rule of the United States government. For eighteen years an army of three thousand men was constantly employed in an effort to keep Navahos and Apaches from molesting white settlers and traders. Finally, in 1863 Brigadier General James H. Carleton, then in command of the territory of New Mexico, announced that there would be no more treaties. Carson then went out and killed their sheep, destroyed their crops, pillaged their land. In 1864 the Navahos surrendered and were given about twelve square miles of land between the San Juan River in New Mexico and the Little Colorado River in Arizona.

The tribe now has a president, annual councils are held, and the Indians are trying in an intelligent manner to get more land, which they really need and which they deserve, for they are good citizens, making their own way without help, living their own lives in the ways of the ancients.

Today the Navaho baby comes into the world, just as he has for centuries, in a dark hogan. There are a midwife to care for him and his mother and a medicine man to chant the proper songs. Parents are most indulgent to their children as they grow up, but early teach them to care for the sheep, which are really the center of the Navaho family's existence. Theirs is a roaming life. Though they seldom travel beyond a ten-mile area, they must constantly move from water hole to water hole, from pasture to pasture, so that their sheep may live.

Little Navaho boys and girls become shepherds almost from the day they start to toddle. They love their little charges with the passionate devotion white children give to their dolls and dogs. And every little lamb is as much an individual to them as are the pets of white children. Out of a flock of several hundred seemingly exact duplicates, every little shepherd can unerringly pick a favorite. It is not unusual to see boys of ten, twelve or fourteen caring for a flock of a hundred sheep, with only a dog to help fight off the coyotes.

The sheep was the gift of the Spaniards in 1540. Until the coming of the conquistadors it was unknown. Before that time the only fibers for weaving were cotton (both brown and white) and the fiber of the maguey. But the Navaho was quick to appreciate the value of the sheep and immediately traded for them—or stole them—and then defended the flocks so efficiently against the Spanish attack that the Pueblo people were forced to come to them to get new flocks.

The Navaho sheep are of a peculiar breed. Their origin is a mixture of many origins. They are small; their fleece seldom weighs more than two and one half to four pounds, as compared to the six- or sixteen-pound fleece of other breeds. Their diminutive size and remarkable sturdiness enable them to roam far in search of pasture and water, and they have developed a phenomenal resistance to sudden changes of weather. The staple of their fleece is not so crimpy as that of the Merino, and therefore it is easier to card and spin. It is long, wavy and relatively free from grease, an important factor when wool must be dyed in a land where water is scarce and arduous to transport. About twenty per cent of the Navaho flocks are sold each year for meat, which is unusually tough. About seventy per cent are sheared and their wool sold. The fleece of the remaining ten per cent is kept for weaving.

The sheep are the property of the Navaho women, not of the men. For in this tribe the woman is the head of the family. She owns the home, the children, the sheep, and when she tires of her husband she has but to say so and out he goes. But she must care for the children, do the cooking, keep two or three rugs going, dye her wools and, if youngsters are scarce, take her spinning with her and go out to tend the flocks. The squaw even takes part or directs the dipping of the sheep and helps with the shearing. A characteristic custom with the Navaho is that no attempt is made to keep the fleece whole. The best parts for weaving are the wool on the shoulders and sides. The fleece becomes coarser toward the tail, and the wool on the belly is worn and dirty, while that on the throat and head is short and wiry.

After the shearing, all other processes in the making of the blanket revert to the squaw. She cards and spins the wool, prepares the dye, chooses the poles and stones to set up the crude upright loom which has not changed for more than four hundred years. She sets up the warp, creates the design, weaves the blanket, carries it to the trader, makes the sale and invests the proceeds. There is no society where woman has higher recognition and none in which she works so hard.

Weaving was not originally a Navaho art. They learned it from the Pueblo people, probably from the Hopis, who are known as the tailors of the Indians of the plateau district.

When the Pueblo people learned to weave is not known, but the legend is that the Spider Woman drew some cotton from her side and instructed a squaw to make a loom. The cotton warp was made of spider web. The upper cross pole was called the sky cord, the lower cross pole, the earth cord. The warp sticks were made of sunrays; the upper strings, fastening the warp to the pole, of lightning; the lower strings, of sun halo; the heald was a rock crystal; the cord-heald stick was made of sheet lightning and was secured to the warp strands by means of rain ray cords.

The batten stick was also made of sun halo, while the comb was of white shell. Four spindles or distaffs were added to this, the disks of which were of cannel coal, turquoise, abalone and white bead, respectively, and the spindle sticks of zigzag lightning, flash lightning, sheet lightning and rain ray, respectively.

The dark-blue, yellow and white winds quickened the spindles according to their color, and enabled them to travel around the world.

Today the Navaho squaw sets about weaving blankets much as you do your knitting. It is no businesslike nine-to-five procedure but a now-and-then method. She weaves

75

between housekeeping and shepherding chores, and the preparations to weave are even more tedious and arduous than is the actual work of weaving itself.

First of all, the wool must be carded to secure a strong, slender thread and to arrange the fibers so that they can be easily spun. There are no known aboriginal tools for this purpose, and so it is supposed that the tow cards were introduced by the Spaniards. They are rectangular pieces of wood with one side covered with leather containing wire teeth. The wool is drawn between the two cards with a pulling movement that is tiresome and hard on the hands. Oftentimes, a group of Navaho women will have a carding bee and get much work done together while their chatter and gossip make them forget their unpleasant task. When the wool has been carded into strips about four inches wide and seven inches long, with all the fibers lying parallel, it is ready for spinning.

The distaff used by the Navahos has a small circular whorl. It rests on the upper part of the leg and is revolved with a twirling motion of the thumb and forefinger. There must be perfect co-ordination between wool, hand and implement.

The success depends largely upon a fine sense of balance and feeling. Spinning is a graceful art, but so tedious and slow are the continued stretching, twisting, winding that it literally wears the fingers to the bone. The ultimate quality of the blanket depends largely upon the perfection of the yarn, and a good spinner enjoys the admiration of all. Years of practice as well as a natural aptitude are needed to become a good spinner of the strong, even, bristling wool twine that weaves so well.

While the work of preparing the yarn goes on, certain dyeing processes are also started. For though the Navaho uses no patterns or copies, she seems to have a clear mental conception of exactly what design and coloring the blanket is to have before she begins to weave it.

During the last decade there has been a revival of vegetable dyes. If you talk with the Navahos about dyes you will now and then surmise that they know and understand the rudiments of chemistry, but more often than not their reply to your queries will be, "I will show you," rather than an explanation. Regardless of any chemical information they may have acquired from practical experience, their knowledge of what can be done with earth minerals, herbs, berries and twigs confirms the fineness of their culture.

When the Navahos first began to weave wool, they had a red, a yellow, a black and probably a blue dye. They also had green. The Spaniards brought them two valuable materials, baize and indigo.

The old blankets have come to be known by the name *bayeta,* an Indian equivalent of "baize." They are characterized by a soft rose-red color of stained-glass brilliancy. This magnificent color was obtained by unraveling and then spinning a European flannel called baize. Just how this material found its way from Europe to Mexico and thence to the distant plateau of the Navahos is a saga of trade that must be replete with adventure. But when burros, horses or men carried baize into Navaho-land, the squaws were quick to seize it, and the glorious color of these prized blankets is proof of their incredible wisdom. Baize was sold until about 1920 by the L. Lorenzo Hubbell Trading Post at Ganado, but it has not been extensively used for the past thirty years.

The first depreciation of the Navaho blanket came with the introduction of machine-spun Germantown yarns. At first these were vegetable-dyed, but soon anilines were used. They had the value of widening the color scheme and of not crocking when washed, but this advantage is questionable in view of the softer colorings of the vegetable dyes, which grow old gracefully.

The Navahos adopted the anilines readily. They were introduced to the plateau about 1886 and were indeed a godsend to a country so lacking in water, but their popularity has greatly diminished. One commercial firm now makes a series called "Old Navaho Dyes," which are now considered good by the Indians and used by them.

The indigo brought by the Spaniards is still in use and is treated—secretly it is said—as it was when it arrived. Urine is used as a mordant, and to this day many Navahos believe that only the urine of a virgin should be used. That of an adult will cause the dye to fade and streak. In this mixture, the yarn is allowed to remain about fifteen days.

A blue dye is also secured by boiling large quantities of larkspur petals with rock salt for about fifteen minutes. The alfalfa is also a favorite flower used to produce this color.

In the old bayetas one frequently sees a beautiful old-gold color. This is still made from the roots of the sorrel, commonly called canaigre. To make this dye, the root is crushed into a paste on a metate. While it is being ground, almogen is added for a mordant. The cold paste is then rolled between the hands into the wool. If the color is not readily accepted, a little water is sprinkled on the wool and the paste, and then all is slightly warmed. In about an hour the wool takes on a rich gold shade.

Yellow is also made from the flowering tops of the rabbitweed, called kay-el-soly (Bigelovia gravealano), which grows plentifully on the prairies and is a member of the aster family. The flower clusters are put in a pot of water and boiled for five or six hours. Meanwhile, a native alum (almogen) is heated in a frying pan until it becomes a paste and then is added to the liquid to act as a mordant. If the unwashed wool is boiled in this mixture for fifteen or twenty minutes, it comes out a shade from canary to a deep old-gold or even an olive-green. A yellow dye is also made from the parasite, mistletoe.

The Navahos make a beautiful, clear, dark, rich brown by boiling the shells of walnuts and a lighter brown by boiling walnut twigs. They use a rich reddish brown which is made by boiling the mountain mahogany with juniper or spruce branches. This they fix with rock salt.

One of their most beautiful colors is a deep, dark purple. This combines indigo with red, which is boiled for about fifteen minutes with the petals of the flower known as four-o'clock. Rock salt is used as a mordant. Their greens are invariably yellowish and are secured by mixing indigo with a yellow dye.

Now that baize is no longer used for red, a rose color is secured from the same red ocher that is used in their sand paintings. A deep cardinal red is made from the ripe prickly pear, a cupful of rock salt and a handful of the barks and roots of the Colorado spruce, steeped in a couple of gallons of water. The rich red dye that most nearly approximates the color in the old bayetas is made in a most arduous way.

First the squaw dusts off a large rock and builds a fire on it with sticks of the juniper tree, called kat. Branches are continually added until a satisfactory amount of ashes is accumulated, when the fire is permitted to go out. The ashes, called Day-Deed-Lit, are collected, rolled up in a cloth and put away. Then the roots of the mountain mahogany (cercocarpus parvifolius) are stripped of bark by pounding them with a flat stone. The roots, whose bark has been loosened by the pounding, are boiled in a kettle for several hours. Meanwhile the bark is pounded into a powder, then pulverized like corn on a metate, swept into a pile and put beside the juniper ashes. Then the entire mess is boiled for about ten minutes, and the dyeing begins.

One of the most frequently used colors in the Navaho weavings is black. This is really a tannic ink called Eel-gee-Bay-tah. To make it, the squaw puts a pot of water over a fire of greasewood branches and fills it with the twigs and leaves of aromatic sumac twisted into bunches about six inches long. This is left to boil for five or six hours. Meanwhile, a second fire is built, and over it yellow ocher, powdered by grinding, is put into a frying pan and roasted until it becomes a dull red. An equal quantity of piñon gum is then added to the ocher, and this mixture is stirred until it becomes a paste. Soon the gum carbonizes and combines with the ocher, forming a black powder.

Then the twigs are taken from the pot and the contents of the frying pan dumped into the liquid, which really becomes an *ink*. Into this the wool is placed and allowed to boil. Buckskin and leather for bridles and saddles are also treated with this dye, which gives a rich and practically indelible black.

The Navahos are firm believers in signs, charms, spells and even witchcraft. Their traditions are rich in beautiful, quaint legends. Their religion is chiefly nature worship, and the colors which they use in their weavings are symbolic of the childlike beliefs of this old race.

To the squaw who squats in the shade of any old cottonwood tree and weaves her yarns back and forth, red is the color of the sun. Warm, vital, life-giving. White is the color of the dawn, of the east. Yellow suggests the glow of the sunset, blue is the color of the south, and black is not symbolic of death and despair, but of joy and hope. It suggests the dark, heavy rain clouds of the north that bring life and refreshment to growing crops and dry springs. So the squaw dips her wool into these colors of earth and sky, of hope and fertility, and trusts that her gods will see and heed.

And now with her yarn carded, spun, dyed, her warp set, it is time to set up the loom.

The squaw appears to be stoical, philosophical until it is time to choose the sticks and stones needed for the loom. Then she becomes as finicky and wary as a race horse at the starting post. She is more particular than a prima donna selecting the costume for the big scene, more exacting than a movie director developing a budding star. But finally sticks and stones are assembled to satisfaction, and the loom is erected with the aid of native rope and stones. It stands upright, and the squaw sits on the ground to weave upward.

Her most precious tool is her batten stick. A weaver will not part with her batten stick any more than a potter will give up her polishing stone. Generally, the stick is a piece of scrub oak about three feet long and three inches wide with boat-shaped ends and thin edges. The skill with which this is pressed down on the warp determines the firmness of the blanket.

Some weavers prefer the comb to the batten because it does not put so much strain on the wool and therefore results in a stronger rug. The combs are usually short and heavy and a word much among the weavers is *Yego,* meaning "bring comb down hard." This is important, for the result is a tension that insures straight edges, an essential quality of a well-woven rug.

Shuttles are seldom used. If many colored threads are

required they are sometimes wound on twigs. Usually the wool is rolled into soft little balls, and with these the swift brown hands work out the pattern that is in the mind.

The designs of today differ from those of the past, when borders were never used. Then it was considered bad luck for the weaver to "weave herself in," and the designs were elongated but never closed.

The designs may be classified into three groups. The early blankets have bands and stripes at top and at bottom, with a wide, more elaborate band in the center. These stripes may also be arranged evenly, top and bottom, with all stripes the same size. The second group consists of blankets with an allover design. This may be a large diamond with terraced borders repeated over a large surface. Within the large design there is oftentimes a smaller diamond. In the third group the entire surface is composed of small triangles or parallelograms of many colors. Sometimes the blanket has a background of zigzags, diamonds, diagonal stripes.

These are the three usual design types, but a fourth may be added—the chief's blanket. The older ones are woven in blue or black or blue and white or a combination of these three colors. In the center will be a large diamond with terraced sides. Each corner will have a quarter of this same pattern. The blankets will be woven so that when the four corners are folded in, the corner diamonds will coincide with one in the center. These chief's blankets are usually one and one eighth to one and one half times as long as they are wide. The stripes of the background run horizontally, which gives impressive height and dignity to the wearer.

A study of Navaho textile designs employed today indicates that they are borrowed from those used in basketry and pottery. You see the same squares, diamonds, sometimes elongated and sometimes joined. The Roman, the Maltese cross, St. Andrew's cross and the triangle appear in many ways. Sometimes squares and diamonds have a serrated edge. Sometimes they have a lace edge. The battlement design and cluster of round and elongated dots are also introduced. Perhaps the best known design is that of terraced clouds and that of the swastika or "rolling logs in a river." This design, now so familiar in Europe, was in use freely all over America in preconquest times. It also appeared among the ancient mound builders of Ohio and Tennessee. Undoubtedly it is the oldest cross in existence and has been considered as a sign of long life, good fortune and good luck.

Whatever the designs may be, they are invariably remarkable for their geometric character and for their lack of realism. And now we come to the often discussed question of symbolism. What do these designs mean?

The extensive research of the celebrated anthropologist, Dr. Boaz, convinced him that all tribes had names for their designs, usually derived from some familiar object. These names might have been given when the designs were truly pictographic, and there is no proof that the decorations were not copied from nature. Few of them are as clearly defined, however, as the cloud terraces of the Pueblos or the swastika of the Navaho.

As to the religious significance of the symbols—the religious art of the Indians was quite realistic, and few Indians even to this day will dare to weave the Mei, the symbol of their God, into a blanket. Therefore, it is clear that *religious symbols stand quite apart from ordinary decoration and that their designs were primarily decorative, though upon them a symbolism was grafted.*

I have come to the conclusion after talking with many who have spent a lifetime studying the Navaho blanket that the true estimate of these designs was given by Father Berard when he said:

There is no system as to the use of the different figures; i.e. they are not arranged into any kind of hieroglyphic order by which a woman could weave her life's history, or any other history or story, into the blanket, as has been asserted by some writers. The Navaho blanket, therefore, is a human document only insofar as it shows the untiring patience and diligence, the exquisite taste and deftness of a semibarbaric people and the high art and quality of their work, wrought with simple tools and materials.

Design in Navaho blankets, like the silhouettes of Parisian *couturiers,* may fluctuate overnight. However, among the products of the Navahos the essential characteristics remain unchanged. There are always the same coarseness and crudeness of material; the same simplicity of design, alike on both sides of the weaving; the same kinds of color.

Today, the art of weaving among the Navahos has progressed to excellent standards. It is true that the old bayetas are no more. It is true that use, and hard usage at that, makes for satiny textures and softer coloring and that, as in wood and metals, nothing can take the place of the patina of time in weavings. But good influences are at work in this field of Indian art.

In the later years of the nineteenth century the demand for the Navaho blanket was such that the Indian traders could not get sufficient supplies. Then the squaws learned that inferior blankets brought money more easily and more quickly. So they speeded up. The inevitable inferiority resulted.

Other detrimental influences also occurred at this time. In 1875 Germantown yarns were introduced. At first these were vegetable-dyed and gave a wider color range, but soon they were colored with aniline dyes, and these same dyes were made available to the Indians. Then came the introduction of cotton warp, and finally, the Navaho blanket became a loosely woven thing, usually of cotton, aniline-dyed.

The traders were first to see the error. Poor blankets brought quick money, but lack of quality soon decreased the demand. Business declined. The traders could read the handwriting on the wall and quickly took steps to repair the damage.

A leader in the revival was Fred Harvey. Today, the greatest collection of Navaho weavings in the world is in the Harvey House in Albuquerque. They rank in beauty of texture, color and design with the masterpieces of foreign looms.

Following the leadership of Fred Harvey, the Indian traders set up new standards. Cotton warps were taboo. Standard colors were approved. The Indians were urged to improve their wools, to invent pleasing designs, to weave tightly, closely and carefully.

Good weavers were shown the fine old blankets and encouraged, not to copy, but to go and do likewise. Good materials were "advanced" to them. The traders even offered prizes for exceptionally fine pieces. Fairs and feasts were held once a year at which exhibitions of good work were placed on view. And, more practically, the traders let it be known that a good price awaited every good weaving. American collectors bolstered up the movement with ready funds for purchasing. And a great American art was saved.

Now you may write or visit the trading posts of Arizona and New Mexico and obtain a Navaho weaving for every purpose. There are rugs, couch covers, runners, pillow tops. The colors are usually black, gray, white, red, though it is possible to secure some blankets colored with modern vegetable dyes of soft rose, green, pink, blue, yellow, purple.

Three grades are made. These are known as common, standard, and extra. When you buy, the reliable trader will point out the size and quality of the warp and of the woof and weft. He will invite you to judge the quality and harmony of color, the originality and attractiveness of design and finally the firmness and regularity of the weave.

When you are making your selection, consider also the *straightness* of the piece. It should lie flat on the floor and be even in width. Its edges must be parallel, and its colors must be the same throughout the length of the piece.

Then hold the weaving up to the light. The web should be of even thickness. The lines of the weaving should be straight. Their uniformity indicates well-spun yarns.

You will, of course, see some minor marks such as the small holes of the needle, or a ridge made by poles, if the rug is over three feet long. Sometimes the thread may stop and turn back in its course. This is a flaw assuredly, but it tells a delightfully human story. Perhaps the sun sinking in the west sent a ray into the eye of the weaver or a hurt child came to be comforted, and her fingers forgot their course; perhaps some weaker muscle in the toil-weary body pleaded for an instant's comfort, and the sensitive brown hands responded. Such imperfections make for more beauty than does the flawless precision of the machine. They cause the thing itself not only to appeal to the intellect and to the senses, which alone machine-made products can do, but to speak the heart. The machine may thrill the mind; the hand makes captive the heart.

CHAPTER SIX

The Navaho Silversmith

WHILE his squaw cares for the children, tends to her house, spins and dyes her yarn, weaves it into blankets and sells them, the Navaho roams the range tending the sheep, a lonely, lazy life which he loves, and works a little silver.

He obtains the money for the silver coins and tools necessary for this work by trading horses at the posts and with the crowds who assemble for the long and frequent "sings" which are so important to his tribe.

The silverwork of the Navaho is the one primitive art which has improved with the years. It has been helped by the introduction of tools from Mexico and America, though perhaps the greatest boon to the Navaho silversmith is emery paper, which has to a great extent taken the place of the crude stones and sands formerly used for finishing and polishing.

Today the Navaho makes buttons, beads, pins, rings, necklaces, earrings, belts, bridle ornaments, boxes, the ubiquitous ash tray and occasionally beautiful tobacco cases. His pieces are distinctive in shape and design because they are inspired by the terrain about him and by his deities. He also draws heavily upon the motifs used both in the decoration of pottery and in the weaving of blankets. These designs are worked into his pieces with a restraint and a dramatic effectiveness that equal that of the master smiths of all times; yet the Navaho works with only the crudest of tools. A low forge, a bellows, an anvil, some tongs, scissors, pliers, files, cold chisels and perhaps a crude matrix or die for molding the buttons. He has a basin; materials for soldering, blowpipe, wire, sandpaper, emery paper, powdered sandstone, boxes, ashes and some dirty rags. For whitening, he uses a native mineral substance called almogen, or salt water.

The Navaho forge may be built of old boards and mud, with a bellows attached. The bellows is a goatskin bag, about twelve inches in diameter, tied at one end to a nozzle and at the other end to a circular disk of wood which serves as a valve. This disk has two arms, one below and one above the handle, with two or more rings of wood placed in the tube to keep it distended. These wooden hoops or rings keep the bellows divided into compartments and thus help to govern the release of air. The nozzle consists of four pieces of wood tied together and rounded on the outside so as to form a cylinder about ten inches long and three inches in diameter, with a quadrangular hole in the center about an inch square. The bellows is worked by horizontal arm movements. Some of the Navahos also buy in the stores cheap bellows such as we use at our fireplaces.

The anvil is any old piece of iron of suitable strength and shape. It may be the wedge or bolt from an old wagon. Even hard stones are sometimes used when iron is not to be had.

The crucibles are made of clay. Molds are cut from soft sandstone to an approximate shape of the article to be made. From the white people come files, scissors, tongs, boxes and awls. Their cold chisels the Navahos make themselves. A piece of brass tubing about a foot long, slightly tapering and curved at one end, serves as a blowpipe, and when soldering is to be done, old rags soaked in mutton fat are set afire to give the needed flame.

The silver is bleached by heating it at the forge and then boiling it in water containing almogen, or salt. When subjected to this ordeal it becomes white in a short time.

The Navaho builds the fire the night before he plans to work on silver. It is kindled of juniper at sunset, and after it is allowed to flame high, it is smothered with earth and left to cool. The charcoal is ready for use the next morning.

Soon after sunup the Navaho is at work. He sits on the

ground with legs outstretched and beats Mexican dollars to about the right thickness, then cuts them with scissors to the desired size and hammers them into shape. Sometimes he molds them with a matrix and then resorts to hammer, chisel and awl. No dividers, squares or compasses are used, though sometimes patterns are cut from paper or scratched on with awls. Yet every piece is a work of art.

A number of the most frequently used motifs from pieces of Navaho jewelry are shown on page 204, together with the names which suggest the meaning of each symbol. However, it is impossible to evaluate the beauty of Navaho jewelry merely from seeing these designs. The beauty of this jewelry rests in the combination of motifs on a piece and in the artistry with which the entire design is conceived and wrought.

In buying Navaho jewelry, as is true in the purchase of silver of all kinds, the weight is one indication of value. The beauty of the design is most frequently to be judged by its simplicity, by the economy of decoration. The better pieces are almost invariably the simplest. Finally, the finish of the piece, its smoothness, its color, its texture, must be considered. As you become acquainted with the jewelry, you will come to recognize the *authority* possessed by the better pieces. The sketches on page 205 are the best definition I can offer for this term, so important in this fascinating art.

The monetary value and sometimes the beauty of Navaho jewelry is enhanced by the use of turquoise,

petrified wood and, infrequently, coral. Turquoise is to
the Navaho what jade is to the Chinese. He loves its color,
its luster, and to him it is a portent of good fortune. Soon
after a Navaho baby is born, bits of turquoise are inserted
in its ears to insure long life and happiness, and the
Navaho loves to embellish his silverwork with this sky-
colored stone. It finds its way into rings, bracelets, necklaces, buttons and sometimes into bridle ornaments.
There is a saying in Santa Fé that if a visitor does not
begin to wear turquoise within a few days after arrival,
he will never return.

Coral finds its way up from Mexico, and beads of coral
are often combined with silver and turquoise into necklaces. I have a long rope of them which I bought from a
Navaho near a trading post. It winds around my throat
about fourteen times, like a *lei*. I paid nine dollars for it.
After I bought it I was curious to know what the Indian
would do with the money. I followed him and saw him
stalk into the trading post and buy nine dollars' worth of
canned beef. One hogan would be the scene of a feast that
night!

Navaho jewelry is suffering now from an epidemic of
commercial imitation. There are several "factories"
which produce these imitations and sell them to stores
and shops and railway stations. They even have represen-
tatives vending their products on railway trains. A quick
way to recognize these imitations is by the clasps on the
pins and the screws on the earrings. No Indian, with his
crude tools, could ever produce such perfect gadgets.

There are also many pieces of exactly the same design, such as the thunderbird or the horse. All of them exactly alike—no Indian would endure the boredom necessary to such quantity production. Upon closer inspection you will find that the designs on these imitations are not etched deeply and are set and even, sure proof that they were stamped out by tools. Price is another indication of imitation. To catch the customer, imitations are usually priced at about one half to two thirds the price of handmade jewelry. The customer thinks he is getting a bargain, but he ends by being cheated.

So prolific is the production of imitation Navaho jewelry that it is wisest now to make your purchases only in reputable shops. The owners of these shops know the Indians who are the best artisans, and the Indians in turn know that there is a ready market and a fair price to be had from these reputable traders, and they dispose of their best work to them. You enjoy the benefit of this mutual confidence. The price may be a few dollars higher, but at most it will be amazingly little for the beauty of the design and the fine workmanship that wrought it.

And it is most satisfying to discover how Navaho jewelry now fits itself into one's costume. The buttons the Navahos hammer and etch for their blouses can be mounted on earscrews and make handsome earrings to wear with sports costumes. They have the dull rich luster of pearls. To women growing gray they are most becoming. The silver beads the Navahos make are perfect to round off the neck of a sweater, and their simple pins and bracelets are effective with sports and daytime clothes. A plain black dress worn with turquoise earrings, bracelet and ring takes on a dramatic interest. Because these simple and effective pieces suit everyday wear so perfectly it is amazing how devoted you become to them. And Navaho jewelry of good design and workmanship is sure to increase in value. I was convinced of this when a ring I bought for six dollars in Santa Fé was some years later stolen from me in a London hotel. I found it some months later in a pawnshop in Kensington, priced at five pounds ten shillings—then about twenty-five dollars. Europe appreciates Navaho silver!

PART TWO

THE POPULAR ARTS OF MEXICO

A HERITAGE OF BEAUTY

INDIAN COLONIAL ARTS—LACQUER

POTTERY—WEAVING

CHAPTER SEVEN

A Heritage of Beauty

IN MEXICO every Indian is an artist. The beautiful things he uses every day are made by hand with an imagination kindled by the green of cedar and pine, the blue of the sky, the white crests of the mountains, the scarlet of the hibiscus and poinsettia, the rose of the sunset on the circling hills and enriched by a tradition that progresses victoriously through centuries of conquest and of depression.

Despite the holocaust to which the Indian of Mexico has been subjected, his basic ideology, his habits and beliefs have not been touched and are expressed every day in the popular arts of this amazing country.

His inherent good taste has come through the churrigueresque period introduced by the Spanish and still expresses itself in what he makes to use. To the Indian woman a pot to store mescal, a jug to carry pulque to the men in the fields is not enough. Her clever hands and beauty-pregnant brain mold that pot to lines that sing with beauty, and with a crude pit of quartz, she etches upon it lovely designs she sees about her—flowers, animals, hills, valleys.

Sooner or later every product created by the Indian's amazing, dexterous brown hands finds its way to the shops along the Avenida de Madero. This street is the Rue de la Paix, the Fifth Avenue, the Unter den Linden of the Mexican capital. It begins at the Zocala and runs westward the length of a beautiful park—the Alameda. It is a narrow thoroughfare teeming with automobiles, honking and fuming resentfully at their retarded progress. Both sides of the street are lined with shops that are crammed with the popular arts of the country. Their windows and shelves are filled with objects of beauty and with objects of superlative ugliness. All are given an equal chance to win the approval and purchase of the hordes of Americans who come flooding through this narrow thoroughfare like cattle through a shed. On every corner, in every vacant doorway, on both sides of the street, vendors hawk their wares, which vary from the well-known scarves of Mexican drawn work to American-made flashlights.

The sight of these poor Indians peddling their wares often makes of one's first impression of Mexico City a nightmare. A government eager for tourists might consider it wise to take these victims out of sight and pension them in a hospital. But not so Mexico. One wonders if she willfully permits these people to remain at large that she may flaunt her wounds in the face of visitors to force home a realization of the wrong that has been done the Indian, who, though conquered, yet remains invincible. For the culture of the Indian of Mexico, despite conquest, ravishment and revolution, still flourishes. His brown hands still possess the power to produce beauty that amazed Cortez and his soldiers four hundred years ago.

When these conquistadors arrived, they were greeted by a people dressed in magnificent mantles of woven feathers, tunics of sumptuous weavings, adorned with gold and precious stones, carrying flowers in their hands. They saw a city encircled by snow-crowned mountains, with three great causeways crossing two lakes that separated into numerous canals and made of it a fairyland that sparkled in the sun, a Venice. These waters were dotted with floating islands profuse with tropical foliage, brilliantly colored flowers and gorgeous birds. More than two hundred and fifty thousand boats moved about on the sparkling waters of these canals, for Mexico City, then called Tenochtitlan, was the capital of a monarchy of about forty million prosperous people with a finer culture than Europe knew.

Its magnificent temples were built of stone and surrounded by massive sculptured walls. Dazzling white palaces were adorned with hanging gardens, lush and tropical. When Cortez was led within them, he found great rooms with walls decorated with tapestries and mosaics. The floors were of marble, the roofs supported by lustrous onyx columns; the furnishings were gorgeous, the baths, luxurious. Bernal Diaz, chronicler for the conquistadors, recorded, "It is like the enchantments they tell of in the legends of Amadis. Are not these things a dream?"

Here on the southern reaches of the Great Plateau the fine arts of sculpture, architecture and painting flourished, though they were unknown among the peoples toward the north. Religion was a powerful force, just as it was and is among the Pueblos. Though the Aztecs and Mayans knew neither bronze nor steel, they were masters of sculpture and of building. In the valley of Mexico the architecture emphasized massive planes; in Oaxaca, Yucatan, Guatemala and the lands toward the south, the architecture of the temples was a glorification of design.

These people had developed the art of sculpture until it was strong, vigorous, versatile, competent to interpret them and their relationship to their gods. Individualism, as we learn of it among the Greeks and in these modern days, was unknown. Their sculpture was the work of anonymous craftsmen, a communal production, conceived and wrought to embellish their ritual.

Stone and clay were the medium used, while plastic forms were employed for incense burners, funerary urns and temple furniture. Always the sculpture was remarkable for a detached, impersonal repose and majesty and an absence of the sensual and emotional.

The paintings of the Aztecs and Mayans never achieved the quality of their sculpture. Painting was exercised principally for frescoes and manuscripts. A few surviving frescoes show the use of red, blue, yellow, green paints, made of vegetable and animal dyes, and seem to date from the time immediately preceding the coming of Cortez.

After the wonder of these arts had ceased to thrill the Spaniards, they became fascinated with the crafts and popular arts of these gifted people. The conquistadors never tired of visiting the markets to see the products of the country which were brought in on the backs of the Indians to the great markets, even as they are today.

Weaving was an advanced art, as the elaborately decorated dress in their sculptures shows. They not only used cotton and the maguey fiber but wove magnificent tapestries, mantles, headgear, fans and shields of the brilliant plumage of tropical birds. Fabrics were decorated with embroidery of many kinds, and the patterns were sometimes tie-dyed (like batiks), or stamped on with clay stamps and vegetable and animal dyes.

Wood carving was a favorite craft, but few examples are now to be seen because of its perishable medium. The Indians made musical instruments, helmets for war, and the canes and chocolate beaters that are now to be had in the markets are survivors of a once great art.

The Aztecs also carved in stone. Onyx vases, rock

crystal vases are still to be seen in museums, but examples of this work are usually above the budget of the tourist and available only to the collector for museums.

Their pottery showed an extraordinary development, as it does today. It was the one of the few arts not bound by ritual. In it fancy might be supreme. The fertile imagination of these people did not hesitate to take this advantage. They modeled figurines, spindles, musical instruments, pipes, censers, stamps for adorning cloths and a multitude of charming toys and practical vessels.

The shapes of their vessels were horizontal rather than vertical (as were the Greeks'), and incising and carving were frequently employed for decoration. The painted design on pottery repeated their basketry motifs, just as did those of the Pueblos. Their pottery vessels were augmented by those made of wood, gourds and calabash, beautifully lacquered, but this work was confined to a few states in Mexico only. Tools were marvelously wrought of obsidian. Axes were made of jade, and arrowheads were of a finer workmanship than the tribes to the north showed. Mirrors were made of obsidian, since glass and bronze were unknown and copper was never used for this purpose.

But it was the ornaments of the Aztecs and Mayans that did most to arouse the cupidity of the Spaniards. Their work in gold and jade has almost entirely disappeared; the jade lost, the gold, though it was worthy of Cellini, melted in the Spanish pot.

The Aztec and Mayan goldsmiths made necklaces,

rings, massive gorgets, earrings, pendants, ornaments, masks and figurines of wondrous beauty. They seldom worked silver, but they knew how to beat out gold leaf and how to plate copper with gold.

The stone most valued was jade. They also used turquoise, obsidian, rock crystal, emeralds, beryl, carnelian, onyx, opals, amethysts, serpentine, nerite and porphyry. But it was the wondrous workmanship rather than the intrinsic value of metal or glass that gave value to their ornaments. They were masters of mosaic, inlaying shell and wood with gems to make masks and ornaments of rare beauty.

Their shell carvings were delicate and highly decorative, pink, white and the softly mottled brown shells being favorites. It is said by authoritative historians that Cortez took $12,000,000 in treasure from Montezuma and that during his rule in Mexico he sent back to Spain gifts valued at $3,600,000,000. Masters of steel and gunpowder, the Spaniards prostituted a greater culture than they knew.

At that time Mexico City was the most beautiful city in the world. Today it is a monument to foreign cupidity and to Indian vigor. Rococo palaces along its tree-shaded avenues tell of easy wealth wrung from the despoiled peon by foreigners who came to get as much as they could and give as little in return to the Indian who once owned all.

Where the magnificent Aztec temples once stood now rises the Cathedral. Beautiful without, it knows little of beauty but much of superstition within. Yet you have only to enter for a moment to become aware of a thrilling Presence, intensely real, though intangible. About you the Indians, with shawl-covered heads, with unshod feet, pray to the patroness of their ravaged land, the Virgin of Guadalupe. The air is heavy with the fragrance of withered flowers, the only offering they can bring to her. But there is a Presence here before which the most iconoclastic must bow. Faith—pure, trusting, devout—is here. You feel it. Thus a noble religion warped by greed is justified.

Gaunt modern buildings bristle up all over the city. Before them, on the steps of the opera house, the most horrible mass of marble the modern world knows, the blind, the lame, the victims of the disease which the Spaniards brought, beg pitifully. Along the streets that fork out from the opera house the shops are filled with the beautiful things made by these Indians.

My first introduction to the popular arts of the Indians of Mexico occurred in one of these shops on an evening many years ago. I was making some purchases when Dr. Moisés Saentz came in. We were introduced. I asked his advice on my selections, and he, with old-world courtesy, consented to look at them. My good fortune never ceases to amaze me!

As subsecretary of education, Moisés Saentz traveled from one end of Mexico to another, visiting every town, village and clump of huts. He sought out the Indians who created beauty in clay, wood, wool, cotton. He searched to discover beauty just as did the archaeologists whose spades unearthed the wonders of Chichen Itza, of Mitla and of Monte Alban. But Dr. Saentz did even more, for the art he discovered was a living art, the art of the people. He brought appreciation and opportunity to the living, for it was largely through Dr. Saentz' efforts that the popular arts of Mexico came into a renascence. Soon the government became seriously interested in them. Collections were made and exhibitions were arranged. Dr. Atl published his excellent book, *Les Artes Populares En Mexico,* and Frances Toor began to edit *Mexican Folkways.* The purpose of this magazine was to formulate the new Mexican attitude toward the Indian by making known his artistry.

Mexican Folkways enjoyed a precarious existence, for money was scarce. Oftentimes it seemed that the latest issue was to be the last, but some beneficent Providence was constantly at watch. Frances Toor, editor, writer, photographer, messenger, traveling correspondent, was also a treasurer who misered over every penny of revenue so that another and still another issue might be published.

While others became sentimental, eulogistic about the artistry of the Indian, and expanded their enthusiasm in unproductive jets, Frances Toor quietly, persistently pursued her purpose, regardless of the personal sacrifices that were constantly demanded. And issue after issue of *Folkways* continued to appear.

These little magazines are now documents of value. Simply, factually, authentically, they explain, picture

and place the arts of the Indian of Mexico. Many generations hence, appreciation and gratitude will be paid to
this valiant editor who delivered her message to Garcia.

Frederick Davis, managing director of the department
of popular arts in Sanborn's Drug Store, Mexico, was
the first American to appreciate and popularize the arts
of the Indian, and is one of the many who are fearful of
the future. Fred Davis fears that in another generation
or so the change must inevitably come and the products
of these people may descend to the level of the cheap
wares of Japan and Czecho-Slovakia.

Today, a walk through the shops along the Avenida
de Madero strikes terror in the hearts of all who know
and appreciate the sincerity and simple beauty of the
popular arts of these gifted people. It is the belief of
many who have admired the arts of the Indians that
this indigenous good taste is now in greater danger than
it has ever been. The avalanche of American tourists de-
manding ash trays, zerapes and baskets and offering
ready cash for poor craftsmanship is becoming every day
a greater hazard to Indian art. And the desire to please
is strong in every Indian. Then, too, food costs are rising
alarmingly.

The deluge of Czecho-Slovakian and Japanese goods
that greet the Indians on every street corner and in every
shop is also weakening their natural conception of beauty.
Watch them stand before the windows and sidewalk displays of jewelry and fabrics, eyes glued upon some tawdry object, and you will sense the inevitable change that

will result in the Indians' acquirement of the same bad taste that those who manufacture such wares show. But there are wise forces at work to prevent this catastrophe.

In the little balcony where Fred Davis has established his office in Sanborn's you may sometimes see him showing a lovely old textile or a bit of pottery to an Indian, slowly turning it this way and that before solemn brown eyes that glow from under the big sombrero. The sensitive, strong brown hands reach out to touch, to feel, to appraise, and you wonder just what the Thing is saying to the Indian.

The interview is quiet, gentle, but you feel instinctively that it is as revealing as a candle gleam in a darkened room. "Make something like this," Davis suggests, and the Indian, quick to sense his keen perception and wise gentleness, nods, then rises, shakes hands, comes lightly down the steep, narrow steps, passes out among the hordes of tourist shoppers on the street below and is on his way. And you wonder what is to happen!

A glance at the walls and into the cases in the room suggests the outcome of this interview, which is but one of hundreds that Fred Davis has had day after day for twenty years. For there are zerapes of genuine beauty, there are lacquers of distinctive conception and excellent workmanship, pottery of fine design and form, beautiful things that speak appealingly to seeking moderns. Everyone who is fortunate enough to take possession of these good things will find in them an investment sure to increase in value with the passing years. And to everyone they will bring some message. To me it was not of power nor terror nor religion, but of hands, brown hands, anonymous hands working for beauty, not fame, creating an art not gracious, gentle, flowing, as did the Greeks, but an art that is fierce, brilliant, exotic—like Mexico.

CHAPTER EIGHT

Indian Colonial Arts

THE popular arts of Mexico range over a wide variety of materials because of the amazing abundance of that fertile land and the prolific imagination and manual dexterity of the Indian. Today only four of the preconquest arts are practiced—weaving, lacquer, pottery and basketry. The many other arts such as silver, leather, onyx, tin, furniture, glass are strongly influenced by colonial culture and tourist demand. These flourish chiefly in the capital, Mexico City, and in Guadalajara.

Though Mexico is rich in it, the Indians did not work silver. In fact, it was exported by the Spaniards, and the manufacture of silver articles was actually forbidden. Silver was mined, sent to Spain and then returned to the colonists. Only the Casa de la Monaye was permitted to mint coins and to make a few articles of silverware for the viceroys. I have one of the few silver trays bearing the zigzag mark of this mint. But after 1854, when the yoke of Spain was thrown off, the Mexicans began to hammer this pliable metal into the ornate designs desired by their patrons. You can see them at work now in dozens of silver factories in Mexico City, in Taxco, in Oaxaca and in Guadalajara.

In the heart of Mexico City is a large factory where the silversmiths may be seen—and heard. You enter a shop, its walls piled high with wares, and go on to the courtyard within. Ramshackled sheds of corrugated tin have been thrown up to shade the smiths from the sun. Here work dozens of Indian boys on pedestals that resemble the old-fashioned schoolmaster's desk. On each stand is a big plate of sealing wax, red, black, terra-cotta. With a few primitive tools and a sheet of silver, the silversmith works, never raising his eyes as you approach to watch, for he is paid by the piece.

In this crude way are fashioned rings, earrings, bracelets, bowls, candlesticks, everything from a brooch to a tea set. You walk around among the workers and wonder at the number of designs they carry in their heads, for all come forth full-fledged without benefit of pattern. The only suggestion of a pattern is some few dozen handles for pitchers and coffee pots which hang on handmade nails on the back wall of the patio.

At one side a fire roars. It is for burnishing. Nearby,

small boys are busy polishing, rubbing and chattering. They are the apprentices who aspire someday to become silversmiths. Back in the shop again, you make your purchases, after which the pieces of your choice are weighed on a small scale. For here, contrary to American custom, silver is sold by weight, not by workmanship.

The designs wrought by these silversmiths are colonial. The pieces are rococo in shape and overdecorated. Bulbous roses, giant daisies, serpents, Aztec symbols and the famous calendar are hammered from the silver in garish profusion. Bracelets, rings, pins, bowls, trays, cocktail sets, teapots—all are adorned with indiscriminate opulence. Their texture is shallow, tinlike, colorless. Soon you begin to feel sorry for this fine metal that has been so tortured by misguided industry. However, a new spirit has come into this craft that harkens back to the days before the Spaniards came to prostitute the art of the descendants of the fine Aztec smiths.

Some five or six years ago an American, interested in Aztec design and encouraged by the easy accessibility of silver, started a silver smithy in Taxco. His name was William Spratling, and he was formerly professor of architecture at Tulane University in New Orleans. Visitors, delighted with his choice and accurate designs and with the excellent craftsmanship characteristic of his pieces, told their friends about him. Bill Spratling's silversmiths increased in number as the weeks went by until now ninety-five Indian boys hammer away in the Spratling Studio in the romantic town of Taxco.

Taxco is an Indian village situated high in the mountains a couple of hundred miles from Mexico City. A good road crossing through Taxco from Mexico City to Acapulco has made this town accessible to the American tourists, and now cameones and cars parade through its cobblestone streets every hour of the day and night. The government long ago sensed the unique beauty of this little Indian city built on the hills and adopted it. No house may now be built in Taxco unless it follows the general conception of its native architecture. Today, authors, poets, artists, delight in its meandering cobblestone streets and beckoning vistas that lead out from the plaza.

You need no book to amuse you while sitting in the tree-shaded plaza of Taxco. You yourself live in history more fabulous than fiction. The trees shed a luxuriant shade; the bandstand houses musicians only on Sundays and fiestas, but every day there is much to amuse and interest. Watch the little men in big sombreros and white calzones gambling before the lacy iron gates of the Cathedral. Watch the constant flow of cars and cameones if you will, or live in mind's eye the story of this pastel village on the purple mountainside.

The houses sprawl up the mountain like a parade of cubes, pink and red, blue and red, white and red, then seem to dissolve themselves into the rock. Terrace mounts over terrace, seemingly painted on the sky. Towering above all are the twin spires of the pink cathedral. Over these same stones on which your huaraches rest, traveled

114

Borda and his followers, and even before them came the Aztecs. José de la Borda arrived in 1717 and ordered the building of roads with walls all the way from the capital. Today two of those viaducts still insure passage to the city.

Borda's peons burrowed into the mountain and brought forth a wealth of silver. It seemed that the deeper they dug the higher Borda built. Never did a man have such a passion for building! The rose cathedral was his thanksgiving token to the generous Virgin who guided him to the silver mine, whose entrance is below the main altar. Soon Borda passed on, and the plaza knew little else than the Sunday market of the Indians. But this peace was not for long. For independence was heralded by troops and bands. Then came Porfirio Diaz and his retinue. Revolution followed. Zapata and his cavalry pranced over these very cobblestones which now echo the rattling cameones of the tourist. Artists set their easels here and there. Circuses came to town. But week in and week out the Indians are still coming to market. All day they sit on their little chairs on the cobblestones to buy, to sell, to sleep. Five little apples carefully stacked, a pile of beans, beads of silver, gay-colored baskets marked with the sad word "Requerdo", crudely fashioned bits of silver jewelry, bracelets and rings of silk and straw—all these and more are for sale on Sundays in the Borda Plaza. And of course there is food—tortillas, coffee, chicken, turkey, pigs.

Taxco is a favorite tourist resort and this influx of

visitors has brought fame not only to the town but also to the silver shop of Bill Spratling. Today the output of his studio is shipped to all parts of the world.

Leatherwork was another innovation of the colonials, who needed saddles for their horses. The Indians' amazing manual dexterity soon produced beautiful examples which have now sunk to mediocrity in the purses, boxes, and so forth, that fill the shops in the national capital, but which reached their zenith in the magnificent leather mosaics to be seen at the national museum.

The presence of great quantities of onyx near Puebla and the influx of tourists have combined to produce a prolific manufacture of ash trays, cigarette boxes, inkstands and peon figurines. Tin has followed the same course. About the only pieces actually made and used by the Indians are little lanterns, but it is difficult to find even one of these that does not show some colonial influence. Today ornate candelabra, cocktail trays, place mats, mirror frames are hammered out of tin and bulge the baskets of homeward-going tourists. And baskets are certainly a boon to the tourist. Into them they efficiently pack the hundreds of purchases made in the markets. Perhaps the most popular are those from Toluco which are decorated in brilliant aniline dyes with the figures of mules, birds, cacti. Undoubtedly they serve their purpose. They bring money for pulque and frijoles to the needy Indian and an essential service to the Americano. But beauty of shape, design and quality of craftsmanship

they do not know. The Indian never uses them—a con-
demnation to be considered!

Another craft, generally considered Indian, but actually of colonial origin, is glass. The one and only place in
Mexico where you will find speed and no smiles is the
glass factory in Mexico City which has existed in one
place and has been owned by the Avalos brothers for
four generations.

The door to the patio invariably stands open, and you
go in unnoticed. You walk over piles of straw and alfalfa,
past little parades of jugs and vases and plates, ready to
be packed into crates made of the unfinished branches
of small trees, tied together with rawhide. The packers
squat on their haunches and work quietly and steadily,
their deft hands never harming their brittle wares.

You walk on and pass under a staircase with an iron
railing whose fanciful design, silhouetted against the gray
stone of the building, is as delicate as lacework. Over it,
quantities of giant geraniums dazzle your eyes with their
blaze of brilliant red. At the threshold you pause, suddenly fearful.

In the dark interior, fire blazes in an open furnace
crudely formed of sheets of iron. Running here and there,
fifty or more small boys and men are rushing about with
long iron rods tipped with blazing spheres of glass. It
reminds one of an old-time torchlight parade. But there
is no gaiety here. All is serious, intense.

The glass blowers pass so near that you actually feel
the heat from the burning glass poised on the end of their

iron torches. To and fro, bending, stooping, running, they go, blowing the glass upward as if sounding a giant trumpet, dropping it to sizzle in puddles of muddy water on the earthen floor. The molten mass passes faces, arms, bodies within a half inch. You sense the horror of what those masses of fire would do to flesh if they touched it for an instant, but they never do. The quick, sure movements of the glass blowers is the one Indian characteristic of this place.

Encouraged, you pass further into the dim room and see a gay little altar to the Virgin of Guadalupe, made of blue paper, which stands fresh and new in one corner of the dark room, like a flower springing from dungeon walls. As you cross the room to the altar, you almost fall into a small pit in the floor. Startled, you pause to watch the glass being molded into jars and pots and pitchers, shaped by a tiny little boy of about ten crouched there in the hole.

The blower bends over the pit. The molten mass comes within an inch of the boy's face, but is deftly placed in the crude iron mold at one end of the pit. Meanwhile the boy has covered his dirty little fingers with pieces of newspaper. He quickly presses the hot mold together, then opens it at just the right moment. The blower lifts the glass, now shaped like a pitcher, and dashes back to the furnace. Soon he appears again, running over to the oven at the other side of the room, lays down his object and rushes back to start another pitcher or perhaps a vase.

You now see the lovely shape and color of the object

lying on the crude iron sheet that serves as an apron for the furnace, but only for a moment. Another worker has picked it up with a long iron fork and placed it in the furnace built of handmade brick under which fire flames. Here it is tempered, and then it is ready to go on its way.

In these primitive surroundings is made that most modern of all glass objects—the neon tube. A slight young lad of some sixteen years and his younger helper seem to have made this their specialty. Their skill is miraculous. First, a large cylinder of molten glass on the end of a large iron tube, handled as lightly as if it were only a needle, is rolled on a steel plate that has been placed on a high table. Over and over the blower rolls the fiery mass until it reaches just the right point of elongation— about the size of a tall highball glass. Then he raises it deftly, touches it to a nearby puddle of water and raises it with a single upward sweep of his arm. It is caught and held by his stocky young helper, and for a moment the glass ribbon swings between them like a hammock. Then they step apart.

This seems to be the critical moment. Two pairs of eyes are glued to the garland of glass swinging between the rods. Two bodies are poised as cautiously as acrobats'. From time to time the elder blows on his iron tube gently, but he never takes his eyes from the lengthening ribbon. Then they begin to stretch the glass ribbon by small, almost imperceptible movements of their arms, shoulders, hips, like the movements of Javanese dancers. Suddenly it is finished! You see stretched on the earthen floor at your feet a tube of glass some twenty feet long that does not differ one millimeter in its width. A small apprentice of nine or ten squats on the floor and with a sharp piece of stone and without aid of measure cuts the tube into exact sections about four feet long. Then the blowers dart off to start a new tube.

Over and over this work goes on, for the factory cannot keep pace with the demands that come in every mail. The business is conducted from an old roller-top desk of golden oak in a little office across the patio where birds sing in dozens of cages lining the walls. You sense a pride of ownership in the magnificent pastel painting of the blowing room that hangs over the desk. It is one of the few things not for sale in all Mexico.

These arts in silver, glass, leather, which the colonials introduced and the tourist patronizes, flourish in Mexico, but there still remain the four preconquest arts and the one magnificent art that is no more, featherwork.

When Cortez and his army arrived, they were thrilled by the magnificent clothes worn by the Aztecs. The feathers of tropical birds were woven into their mantles and headdresses, which blazed with color. This feather-work reached its glory in magnificent capes, headdresses and fans, now to be seen in the Museum of the City of Mexico, but today it has deteriorated to nothing more than tawdry birds on bridge tallies, cocktail trays and postcards.

Today the four preconquest arts are still created in hundreds of little dusty, sunny villages, and if you would see them in the making, it is wisest to establish headquarters in four principal cities and from them to motor to the villages. The headquarters for such tours indicate Mexico City, then Oaxaca to the south, Michoacan to the north and Guadalajara to the west. A visit to these centers will give you a thorough idea of the standing the primitive arts now have in modern Mexico. To carry out this plan I have prepared this "work sheet" and I hope that everyone who reads it may have the fun of following this lead.

Popular Art Centers of Mexico

Mexico City

Straw toys, baskets, cooking pottery, leather, furniture, drawn work, sashes, ayates, silver, glass, zerapes, wood carving.

San Angel

Cooking ware, ocher-colored; baskets with designs of lines, birds, messages.

Cuernavaca

Pottery, tinware, sandals, furniture, silver, toys.

Taxco

Jewelry; silver. William Spratling's silver shop is here. Tin, lanterns, frames, etc., colonial influence.

Texcoco

Zerapes with geometrical plant designs, fine texture— colors: blue, tan, brown on white background; pottery; glass.

122

Toluca

Embroideries, sheets, spreads, napkins, table runners, tablecloths, bags; hand-spun cotton embroidered with animals, flowers, birds.

Baskets, heavy, coiled; brilliant aniline colors; flowers, birds, animals, people in stylized designs.

Puebla

Pottery, glazed and ordinary pottery; Talavera tiles, majolica; onyx; polychrome palm petates.

Santa Ana

Zerapes, wool cloth, sashes.

Amazoc

Pottery toys, spurs, bridles of steel and silver.

HEADQUARTERS AT PATZCUARO, MICHOACAN

Uruapan

Lacquer with incrustations of flowers, animals, plants; gourds, calabashes, chests.

Patzcuaro Market

Pottery—some with preconquest faces; copper pots, rebozos, chocolate beaters; zerapes—wools, plain red centers and borders; wool cloth; sashes; jewelry, gold and silver.

Paracho

Rebozos, chocolate beaters, musical instruments.

HEADQUARTERS AT OAXACA

Oaxaca
Pottery, dark-green, glazed; breakfast, luncheon sets; bowls decorated in blue, purple, brown, yellow, red; floral decorations on a cream ground; sienna pottery; jewelry, gold and silver.

Teotitlan del Valle
Zerapes, polychrome with Aztec calendars; stripes with idol in center; cream ground with polychrome geometric designs; sashes and bags.

Azumpa
Pottery, green, glazed; toys and toy dishes.

Coyotepec
Pottery, black unglazed "Gabil" pottery; jugs, jars, bowls, bells.

HEADQUARTERS AT GUADALAJARA

Tepec
Bags and belts of Huichole Indians; beautifully woven patterns of animal and plant designs.

Jalisco
Pottery; blue and blue-gray, unglazed plates, jars, vases.

San Pedro Tlaqueque and Tonala

Pottery, glazed and unglazed; toys, fruits and vessels.

Coatepec

Zerapes in dark, natural wool colors with bright flower centers.

Tuxpan

Cloth, wool, handwoven by women.

POPULAR ARTS PRODUCED IN VARIOUS OTHER STATES

Chiapas

Pottery, bowls painted with gay flower and bird designs on black, green, red, yellow backgrounds.

Textiles, some coarsely woven, some resembling Guatemalan designs.

Chihuahua

Zerapes and sashes, natural wool colors, simple designs.

COAHUILA

Satillo

Zerapes, mostly bad, weaving greatly deteriorated; diamond center, cross stripes, polychrome colors; tin masks.

GUANAJUATO

Guanajuato

Pottery, sienna cooking ware; sets of dishes in glazed greens and browns.

Dolores Hidalgo

Zerapes, coarse but good; rebozos; paper toys.

León

Paper toys and masks.

Celaya

Cotton textiles.

GUERRERO

San Miguel Huapan

Pottery, unglazed, primitive, beautiful.

Olinala

Fine lacquer, old and new; top layer carved to show second color; gourds; calabashes; small boxes of fragrant olinohue wood; chests, conventional designs; some show Oriental influence.

Chilpancingo

Weavings, textiles, sombreros, petates.

Acapulco

Jewelry; gold, filigree designs; colonial influence.

HIDALGO

Ixmiquilpan

Textiles, handwoven; bags; ayates of maguey fiber embroidered with bird and flower designs.

Actopan

Textiles, sashes, ayates, bags.

MORELOS

Queretaro

Otomi textiles, belts, bags, heavy woven baskets, bands and rope; opals; miniature furniture.

San Luis Potosi

Pottery, rebozos, zerapes.

Vera Cruz

Huipils, wool sashes, stone metates, simple pottery.

Yucatan and Tabasco

Hammocks, huipils, pottery, palm hats. Gold filigree rosaries and earrings showing colonial influence can be bought in Vera Cruz.

CHAPTER NINE

Lacquer from Worms and Calabash

THE fine lacquer made by the Tarascan Indians is comparable with the best work of the Orient. This primitive art never ceased to excite the wonder and admiration of the conquistadors, who had never before seen lacquer, and their letters to Spain are filled with its praise.

In 1639, Fray Pablo de la Purisma Concepcion Braumont said in his chronicle:

These Tarascans were the inventors of this painting on wood objects, without imitation until now. It can still be appreciated in the bateas of Periban and in the work of Uruapan, the *lacquer being so constant that it rivals the object in duration and permanence.*

Beautiful examples of lacquer are to be found in the shops of Mexico City, in village markets and even in the hands of vendors along the roadside. To this day lacquer remains one of the finest expressions of the Indian's skill, artistry and tireless patience. There is no primitive art which so graciously conforms to modern ideas of beauty and none which can so readily enter our contemporary homes to lend color, interest and decorative charm, as well as usefulness.

Lacquer is made in Olinala, in the state of Guerrero, and also in Michoacan, a few hundred miles from Mexico City. It is a delightful motor trip, for a good road has recently been completed, to the joy of the American tourist.

The trip to lovely Michoacan is one of rare beauty. Everyone who loves the countryside finds a never-failing source of delight in the sharp tang of its pine forests, the profusion of its flowers and foliage and, always, the encircling hills. Higher and higher the car mounts through the blue and buoyant air as if constantly reaching for that beautiful tissue of sapphire which is the sky. But when you reach Michoacan, still another beauty greets your eager eyes, the beauty of still lakes that reflect in their clear depths forest, mountain, cloud, sky.

The principal city of Michoacan is Uruapan. Among its fifteen thousand inhabitants are a small group of families who have worked in lacquer for generations. They live in a separate barrio or quarter called "la Magdalina" and men, women, little girls, little boys, all do

129

their part in the making of bateas (shallow bowls) and plaques, trays, and boxes.

The shapes of these objects are quite plain but of excellent proportions. The most characteristic object being the batea, a shallow bowl or plaque an inch or two in thickness, slightly hollowed on the top. It varies from a few inches in diameter to a foot or even more. These larger examples are now becoming scarce, as the government is prohibiting the Indians from cutting down the great old trees of which these objects are cross sections of the trunk.

The surface of lacquer ware is decorated until it assumes the appearance of a colorful mosaic. It is carved with intricate designs, then painted in brilliant colors, or sometimes in only two colors, such as red and black, red and white, chrome yellow and black, or green and white. Such color combinations create a contrast that is most striking. The polish is so high that it makes the object appear as luminous as a rare gem. When new, this lacquer glows like a multicolored setting of jewels; when old, its luster dims, its colors fade to the muted richness of medieval stained glass.

These beautiful bateas were originally the mixing bowls for the kitchen. Corn meal, peas, beans were stored in them. Food was prepared and sometimes served in them. But the wonder of their making is no less remarkable than their beauty.

All good lacquer is made with the hands, even to the fine lines which are grooved in with the fingernail. In

Uruapan the process is to lacquer the batea, or box, cut out the designs, which are usually flowers, leaves, birds, then apply one color at a time with the palm of the hand, waiting for it to dry before applying the other color. Then comes the rubbing. Hours and hours of it. Over and over the gay-colored bowl passes the sensitive brown hand. Finally there appears the luminous luster which is the characteristic of fine lacquer.

The Indians of Michoacan use a tree called Tilia o Tzirnu which they dry carefully and then carve. They themselves have named the two operations lacquer and incrustation.

When the bowl or box has been dried and polished to satisfaction, they begin to lacquer it with siza and tzipatz. The siza is a mixture of carbonate of lime, carbonate of magnesia and silex, pulverized and sifted, then saturated with oxide of iron. This mineral is plentiful just a short distance south from Uruapan. Tzipatz is the fat of the aji, a worm. It is prepared by first gathering these worms alive. If they die before they can be brought to the hut, they are considered spoiled. These live worms are thrown into a pot of boiling water which is stirred frequently and quietly with a knife so that the worms do not burn. When they begin to give off a yellowish matter, the pot is removed from the fire and small portions are put on a thin strip of cotton which is placed over the mouth of a jar containing cold water. The mess is stirred in a mortar, a little tepid water being added so that the substance will not harden. Then it is strained and left to cool for a day

131

or two until work starts again. The substance is put in a bowl and beaten, then washed in cold water to clear off a harmful reddish deposit which is inclined to gather. It is then wrapped in maize leaves and is ready to be mixed with aji or cooked linseed oil.

When the object is dried and ready for ornamentation, its surface is evenly oiled with this siza, a fine powder of the desired color is lightly smoothed on, and it is left to dry in the shade. Then the application of siza is repeated, more color applied. Afterward a little oil with drops of tzipatz is added, and again the object is left to dry. Now begins the rubbing which continues hour after hour until a fine luster appears.

Then comes the second step—the incrustation. With miraculous dexterity the design is etched with a fine steel point. Afterward the lacquer is scratched out with a well-sharpened tool until the wood is uncovered. In this hollow, siza is again applied, and the process continues as before. Every color demands this same preparation and procedure, as two colors cannot be worked at the same time, and each one must dry before the next is applied. The final step is rubbing with cotton and a little aji mixed with oil and three weeks may pass before the article is completed.

In the state of Guerrero the little village of Olinala has become the Capital of the Calabashes. There is no more interesting way to spend a morning than to sit with one of the Indian women and watch her convert these crude plants into objects that sing with gay color and challenge you with their vivid designs—one lovelier than another.

Their designs are more conventional than the leaves, birds, animals, seen in Uruapan. Some even show a decided Chinese influence in drawing and in coloring. On my last visit I was fortunate to secure a gourd some fifteen inches in diameter painted a brilliant Chinese red and decorated with pink and blue flowers, with great jade-colored quetzal birds linking beaks around it.

But the most amazing phase of the work in Olinala is not only the design but the source and preparation of the colors used. My gorgeous red calabash bowl was painted with a deer's tail dipped in a powder consisting of equal parts of two earths (called Hexicaltel and Textectl) and a little vermilion, then burnished while still moist with a piece of flint (called Tlaquiltetl.) Every five minutes my bowl was polished by hand, the rubbing being done with a little cotton.

The blue coloring is made in much the same way as the red except that indigo is mixed in with the other earth colors. The yellow comes from cooking a hairy little plant in water and squeezing it with the hands. Then the color is mixed with the powders and again put on the fire and dried to a paste in the sun.

Green is formed of blue and yellow mixed in the proportions which insure the desired shade. Purple is prepared from red and blue. Black is made by mixing the earths Toxicaltetl and Toctetl with charcoal powder, made by burning the heart of an ear of corn. White is merely the mixture of Toxicaltetl and Toctetl without the addition of any other earths.

Here in Olinala incrustation is not practiced. Occasionally, however, slight indentation is secured by grooving with a maguey thorn. Besides the bowls of calabash and gourds, there is a delightful lemon-scented wood used to make little boxes. And there are also large chests similar to the early dower chests of Europe and colonial America.

The old chests are truly magnificent. They are literally on fire with rich, vibrant color. Usually the backgrounds are deep dark blues or rich somber blacks which serve to accentuate the beauty and the brilliance of the design, which is applied in red, blue, yellow, and greens that lean toward the olive and reseda tones. Birds, animals, flowers are combined with rare distinction over the entire surface, both inside and out. If these chests were covered with velvets or brocades they could not present a richer appearance. The modern chests whose colors are newer and brighter are not so lovely to me, but time can remedy this, and others may prefer their freshness.

Lacquer has certain earmarks of distinction no less important than those of pottery, silver or textiles, and it has other characteristics definitely its own. The first requisite is that the piece be in good condition. Sometimes—and this is particularly true of modern lacquer— it is cracked, either from shipment or from handling. This is to be watched against, especially when buying calabash bowls, which are more fragile than those made of wood.

There is not much choice in the matter of shapes. All are simple and good. The three most important considerations to remember are color, design and luster. Of these the latter is most obvious. However, the matter of design can well be summed up in one word, *economy*. Or perhaps *restraint* is the better word. The pattern of fine lacquer is never bold. It is one with the wood or with the gourd. It flows over it easily, gently. It is like a well-chosen dress on a beautiful woman—there, but not obviously so. Such economy insures distinction.

The best lacquer has a very high, even luster which reflects the light no matter how you may turn the object. When deciding upon this quality, you have an unseen guide at your side—the Indian who made it. For if the artist finds that the design and coloring are disappointing, he will not spend a great deal of time on the lacquering and polishing. And the Indian's sense of beauty seldom errs. Trust it!

Two types of design are almost invariably good, and they are genuinely Indian. The first combines animals such as deer, rabbits, squirrels or birds with vines, leaves and conventional motifs. The second consists of flowers, birds and conventional motifs done in a flat style definitely Chinese in inspiration. This latter type of design is usually seen on calabashes, while the former is usually done on wood. Beware the piece that is covered with flamboyant roses and daisies; usually the crudeness with which the *underside* is carved, its feeble luster as well as the poorly drawn pink, white and red flowers that cover it will help you to decide against it.

Occasionally you will see two other kinds of design, one that reproduces the decorations in old illuminated missals. This is most often seen on small boxes and was originally copied by the Indian from the old illuminated missals used by the monks. These designs are very handsome and usually combine blues, greens with gold on black. All have a very high luster.

A very charming design has been recently originated in a little village near Mexico City by a man who is, I'm told, an ex-bullfighter. This design consists of dainty men and women in the costume of 1860 promenading among swans, fountains and trees. The background is an antique white, and the figures are picked out in clear reds, blues, greens, yellow. The luster is quite dull, but suitably so. This design appears on bateas and in boxes of all sizes. I recently saw a beautiful jewel box made to order for an American who cherished beads and rings. The charm and ingenuity with which these baubles were taken care of by numerous trays and partitions, all daintily decorated, were amazing.

This lacquer ware has one quality which immediately endears it to the practical American. It is impervious to water, acid and alcohol. Therefore these handsome bowls and bateas are suitable for table accessories—for salad bowls, fruit plates, centerpieces. The trays can be used for serving both food and liquor. The very large bateas, placed on a simple painted stand of matching or harmonizing color, make handsome coffee tables in the living room or on the porch or even in the garden. The little boxes make pretty containers for jewelry, gadgets and cigarettes. There are bateas too lovely for such practical purposes. These can be hung on the wall to lend all the color and charm of a fine picture.

The large chests placed on low stands are both decorative and practical. They make handsome pieces to hold linen in the dining room or blankets in the bedroom. They are stunning as decoration in that bête noire of the home, the narrow hall. There is no interior too elegant to receive them graciously, none too simple for them to be at home in. The glory of their color, the beauty of their design will delight the eye for longer than any of us may have to see. Of all the primitives of the plateau, lacquer, least known, least appreciated, is best suited for modern enjoyment.

The deterioration of lacquer has now begun. The Indian must have corn, and its price is steadily rising. Along with the increased cost of living has come an unprecedented demand by American buyers and tourists for inferior work. Their demand for quantity rather than quality is sounding the death knell of this original and beautiful Indian art. So the Indian speeds up, and the inevitable deterioration results.

Upon my return to Mexico City after four days spent in this paradise, I watched the sale of lacquer in the curio shops with added interest. Invariably tourists would buy three or even four inferior pieces rather than one good one. I could not but explain this by the Indian's eager desire to please. I knew he would make more articles of doubtful quality, since sales, and therefore money, come more quickly via this route.

All other art objects imported from Mexico and placed on sale in American shops and stores are better chosen than the lacquer ware. Why I do not know, but it is a pity that we cannot have the opportunity to buy the same quality in lacquer that we can buy in weavings and in pottery. Only a few good specimens of lacquer seem to be imported, but this fact adds to your triumph when you are fortunate enough to find amongst the litter a really lovely piece.

Recently I attended in New York City an exhibit of so-called choice pieces of Mexican popular arts, pieces that were supposed to be representative of the finest workmanship of that country. When I saw the lacquer work I was so horrified that I rushed out of the shop. I felt cheated. I felt that great artists had been insulted. Then I went back and bought one piece.

It is overdecorated. Gaudy flowers cover the entire surface, and their size is entirely out of scale with the object itself. The design is carelessly drawn, the lacquer uneven, and too many colors are employed in the painting. The underside of the piece is marred by welts made by the knife in cutting the piece from the tree. It has practically no luster.

I could not help contrasting this ash tray with a

small piece I once saw in the magnificent lacquer collection of Fred Davis. His tiny tray was colored a rich Venetian red, and across its surface a single spray of three delicate leaves had been painted in a reseda green. It was polished to the glow of a ruby.

But the real tragedy of my ash tray is not in its ugliness and careless workmanship but in the fact that it was presented as representative of Indian art.

CHAPTER TEN

The Potters of Mexico

THE finest culture of the Great Plateau flowered in the valley Oaxaca, a few hundred miles southwest of Mexico City. Today the descendants of those great builders, sculptors and artisans make of Oaxaca one of the important art centers in this prolific country. Yet the number of visitors who go to Oaxaca is comparatively few, for the trip is tedious, dirty, hot and uncomfortable.

Oaxaca was founded about the middle of the fifteenth century by Montezuma I, who established his Aztec colony there on the edge of Zapotec territory to protect the trade route to Tabasco. The conquistadors came in 1529, and Oaxaca was declared a city by Charles V in 1532. Here the padres built several fine churches and a monastery whose cloisters are vaulted and ribbed in masterly design. But the story of this valley begins long before the coming of the Spaniards. Toward the south, the Mixtec Indians built the beautiful temple of Mitla. To the west, on a great mountain overlooking the city, the Zapotec Indians built the pyramids and tombs of Monte Alban. Here have been found dazzling riches in jewels, sculpture and paintings. To the archeologist, to the student of the colonial, Oaxaca is a mecca, and to me, whose simple taste delights in the native handicrafts of the Indians, the market and the villages nearby are rich in interest and beauty.

Much of the handicraft made in these villages is carried in on the backs of the Indians to be sold in the market at Oaxaca, which still remains a real Indian market. Toluca's famous market has become as Americanized as Woolworth's now that good roads make it so easily accessible from the capital. The Oaxaca market, too, is doomed to change, but not until a good road to the city makes the trip easy for the tender American tourist.

There is nothing more conventional than a Mexican village unless it be a Mexican market, and Oaxaca is true to type. Since the days of the Aztecs Mexican markets have not changed, except that they occur every seventh day, instead of every fifth day as they did when the Aztecs observed their five-day week.

For ten years I have returned at intervals to the markets in Mexico, and never has the location of the various wares changed. Friends who have repeatedly visited them

141

over an even longer period confirm this same fact. Only recently have the hideous products of Czecho-Slovakia, Japan and the United States crowded themselves into these colorful streets. And what eyesores they are! One shudders for the future! But today the bartering goes on and on, sales are made by the piece or by the pile; the dozen count is unknown, just as in the days of the Aztecs.

A melon, a few sticks of wood, a handful of flowers are all one needs to start up a business of one's own. A few eggs, a few tomatoes, a chicken, at most a few turkeys, herded together like sheep, these are sufficient to bring on foot ten, fifteen, twenty miles to market. And then all the way back again with, if one is lucky, a few more centavos. To sell, to buy, to barter, to exchange, perhaps to visit the church, but even more important to see one's friends—such is the function of the market of Mexico. Trade and religion have been, since the days before time, the reason for meeting the world over. They remain so in Mexico today.

It is never possible to buy or to sell alone. The vendor must have a helper. The buyer must have four, six or a dozen to approve or denounce his selection and offers, to assist him to select his goods, to approve enthusiastically or solemnly register silent disapproval of his choice.

And the small boy is ever-present. He is one of the charms of the land. How he finds you is a mystery, but he never fails. Before you realize it he is standing by your side, first quietly, then possessively. You sort, cast aside, weigh, select, barter. Patiently he waits. If many objects enter into the sale he is all service and attention. He places a little chair or stool for you to sit on. He holds your basket. He arranges and rearranges the wares. The light touch of his small brown hand calls your attention to the better buy. He observes the counting of the change to the centavo. He smiles up into your face in delighted triumph when you win a barter. The hardest heart in the world would melt before the plea of his brown eyes. As he reaches for the basket to carry your wares home, you meekly bow to his wish—though it may mean a toston or even a peso.

When you go to market in Mexico you find first a layer of loiterers and beggars. Men and women squat about and sleepily watch the vendors and buyers. Then there is the street of textiles where rebozos, zerapes, cotton goods, embroidery are sold. There is the street of pottery, where the types characteristic of the towns and nearby villages are ranged in neat rows on the ground. There is the street of flowers and of food raw and of food cooked. One should have only eyes upon entering this section. Noses might well be left at home. The arrangement of the wares reveals a glowing colorful picture at every turn. Purplish red camotes; green papayas; mangoes every shade of yellow and gold; heaps of golden bananas; chili, red, green, purple, black; beautiful pale green anonas. Mounds of roses, heaps of violets, hills of gardenias.

There are mysterious-looking little piles of seeds and grains. One recognizes the ajanjali, used to make mole, the green petitas on calabaza that makes the taste of duck

143

paradisaical. "What are these?" "Dead flies for one's pets, señorita." All is arranged with meticulous orderliness.

Every market has it herb doctor, who is sage, philosopher, prophet as well as doctor. At this booth one can get dead hummingbird bodies for safe journeys. Positive cures for snake bite. Infallible charms to insure, or not to insure, pregnancy. Digitalis for weak hearts. But lest we scoff, we must remember that it was the Indian who gave us this latter medicine as well as quinine and cocaine.

The booths of dulcets are fascinating—until you taste them. Their cloying sweetness is too much for my palate, but the cool pink, green and white ices are most inviting to a parched throat.

There are piles of sombreros house-high, a maze of them from which it surely would require a week to select one. Next to gaudy, garish displays of cheap machine-made cottons are the beautiful hand weavings and embroideries of the Indians themselves. On the cobblestones, earrings, beads, bracelets of the worst Czecho-Slovakian manufacture are invariably surrounded by a silent, eager throng of window-shoppers, or perhaps I should say eye-shoppers. Next to them on the cobbles lie the lace-like filigrees in gold and silver wrought by the hands of ten- and twelve-year-old youngsters, each earring or necklace a gem in workmanship and design made with the timeless patience and acute sense of pattern that bespeak inherent artistry.

Fascinating to me were the junk stalls of Oaxaca, their

walls covered with old iron. Locks, keys, knives, stirrups, belts, chains. Beautiful old keys, practical and proud. Among them I found lovely old saddle buttons and door-heads of steel inlaid with silver that, brightly polished, now give *chic* to my Molyneux coat.

Spanish translations of the classics in soft leather bindings, magnificently tooled—Price? Ten cents, American money. My survey of these was stopped by the song vendor.

A handsome boy with a theatrical tilt to his sombrero, a dramatic fling to his red and black zerape, he plucked out his accompaniment on his guitar to the song frequently named "The Virgin of Guadalupe." Each time the name of the Virgin was sung all sombreros were solemnly raised. All except one. He stood there young, bold, defiant. But when he noticed that many brown eyes were focused on him and one of the owners fingered a machete purposefully, he too raised his sombrero when the Virgin's name was sung.

In the rear of the market are the booths of baskets and pottery—my real reason for visiting this market. By now I must admit that I had completely forgotten that I had a reason, which is typical of what Mexican markets do to you.

Each little stall is surrounded by its wares, arranged with great neatness, in startling contrast to the confusion of sounds and smells.

For Mexican markets are like American five-and-ten-cent stores. You may need nothing when you visit them.

You leave them laden. So many little things beckon to you and for the moment seem absolutely necessary to existence. You wonder why you haven't realized it before, and when you come home and survey your purchases you wonder what you are going to do with them. Where can you tuck them away? To whom can you give them?

It was in this mood that I made my collection of inch-high pitchers, in Oaxaca. Great baskets of them attracted my attention. Their fanciful shapes made me curious to know just how many designs these Indians could fashion, and that curiosity was my undoing!

I knelt down on the cobblestones and started my search. The Indian woman and her husband brought out more baskets of pitchers. He spread a petate on the ground, and we began our search.

"Que bonita, Señorita."
"But see this little one," we laugh gaily.
"Is this one not a beauty?"
"Look—how beautiful, *Señorita.*"

Fragile, delicate as porcelain, the color of the glassy green of seaweed under water; the contents of the baskets were swiftly ransacked by the brown hands, with never a false or disastrous movement. The small boys gathered.

Five little pitchers—ten little pitchers—twenty little pitchers—I counted. Suddenly I thought—how could I carry them home?

The thought barely presented itself to me when one of the lads produced a little basket—just the thing! He began to collect the little pitchers, tucking them in as gently as if they were chicks. We searched for more. Out came more baskets. The exclamations began all over again.

Then the bartering started. For the enormous sum of one peso fifty centavos (less than fifty cents in American money at that time) I had fifty-two lovely little green pitchers, each one a beauty, each one different, and a basket thrown in. We started homeward. Halfway across the plaza I heard bare feet running, a short-breathed panting. I turned. The vendor held a tiny green pitcher in her hand. Sure enough. I hadn't one in all the fifty-two like it! My retinue of youngsters cheered with delight. She had run all the way to bring it to me. She refused money, but I managed to press a flower and five centavos in her brown hand.

"*Gracias, gracias, señorita, muchas gracias.*" And we were all beaming and happy and hot.

For the benefit of those who market according to plan and who do not wish to waste money on buying wares from faraway, I have listed on page 122 the characteristic wares of the principal markets in Mexico. The list may serve as a memorandum to take you to market, but I hope you won't make up a shopping list. Half the fun is in finding things beautiful and unnecessary and desirable and in assembling your purchases before you on your return. Then to admire them, to dote over them, and to silence sternly anyone who dares venture to ask "why?"

In the market at Oaxaca you will see a black pottery called by the Indians Gabil. This is the Zapotec word meaning "hell." Tourists seldom buy it; yet this is one of the few really Indian products without influence of the colonial that is sold there. Today, Gabil pottery is made in the little village of Coyotepec—the hill of the coyotes—exactly as it was before the conquest of Cortez.

Coyotepec lies westward beyond the hills where the Zapotecs built the wondrous city of Monte Alban. This site was excavated in 1910 by Alfredo Caso, and its pyramids have been restored so that it is possible to imagine how glorious this city in the clouds must once have been.

On the main road you follow westward over loose gravel until you reach the imposing plaza about which Coyotepec is built of mud and cacti, but you will not linger. You continue down the streets, along which each little house and plot is fenced with organ cactus, to the home of Junito, the barber and Rosa, the potter. They come to meet you at the entrance, Junito solemn, courteous, Rosa all gaiety and bubbling laughter. You shake hands with each member of the family, and Rosa, as enthusiastically as if you were suggesting a game, agrees to make a pot for you. You enter the patio.

Here at the front of the house Junito has his barber shop. A Standard Oil can serves to hold his tools, the roof of the house projects to furnish a degree of shade, the chairs are made of short boards nailed to an unbarked log. The price is ten centavos for a haircut and ten centavos for a shave if you face the street, or five centavos for a haircut and five centavos for a shave if you face the house. Bunches of black hair strewn profusely over the earth attest the popularity of Junito, the barber.

In the courtyard, drying in the sun, is the earth that soon is to be fashioned into these beautiful bowls and jars. It has been carried in from nearby hills in a petate through which some twigs have been placed so that it becomes a sack. We walk on into the house and sit down on little stools while Rosa begins her preparations.

There is a tall column of black earth, moist and soft in the hut. This is the clay after it has been worked smooth by the feet of the boys. With a kind of saw made by stretching a wire across a small wooden ladder, Rosa cuts from the column the amount of clay desired, kneels on the floor and kneads it as if it were bread—on her metate.

She thumps and pounds away, then balances the hunk of black clay on a couple of broken bits of pottery. She uses no wheel, for the Indians did not know the secret of the wheel when Cortez arrived, and Gabil pottery is made today exactly as it was four hundred and more years ago.

Something of the mystery of this evacuation of time settles on us as we watch those quick, skilled, strong hands. The sun is hot outside, but here in the little thatched adobe hut are the coolness and quiet of twilight. Slap-slap-slap sound those skillful winged hands. Rosa revolves the clay, working with one hand first inside, then out. She cuts a small piece of clay, makes a coil; the coil

149

becomes a neck on the bulbous vase that is now taking shape before our eyes.

Rosa dips a bit of hide into a bowl of water and smoothes the surface to glassy evenness. A few more turns, and then it stands before us—a mescal jar of beautiful shape and proportion.

This jar, like the others that stand on the floor, will be dried in the shade for several days. Then Rosa will etch on its surface with a bit of quartz the decorations that she fancies. A conventionalized rose or a great triangle or a favorite phrase; then it will go to be fired in the crude kiln at the rear of the hut.

The kiln is nothing more nor less than a large hole dug out of the earth and lined with stones. The top is covered with broken bits of refuse pottery. It is fired from below. The poker used to prod the fire is a long branch of a tree with a stone at the end.

The shapes of Gabil pottery are very beautiful. They have the dramatic economy of the functional. There is a small, narrow-mouthed water jug with three rings so that it can easily be carried on the shoulder, a bulbous-necked mescal jug, a round, squat pitcher to carry pulque to the men in the fields, a wide-mouthed vase with perforations to sift corn, and there are charming little bells that ring in clear, flat tones. One peculiarity of this pottery is that it is all made with a round bottom. Little rings are woven of straw to hold the objects in the desired position, the same kind of rings used by the Pueblos.

Gabil pottery calls to mind the black pottery made at

the pueblos of San Ildefonso and Santa Clara in New Mexico, but it is really quite dissimilar. In color it is the same, a sooty-black obtained by the same process of firing—that is, by keeping the pottery covered so that the smoke becomes ingrained with the clay. But in all other ways it is different. The shapes of Gabil pottery are all functional and unique. The pottery is made for use, with no thought of sale to the tourists, while in the pueblos the reverse is true. The Gabil ware is not so carefully polished nor so beautifully decorated, and the bottoms of the pots are always round. A comparison of the sketches of Pueblo pottery shown on page 199 and of Gabil pottery shown on page 208 closely indicates the difference in these seemingly similar wares.

The making of commercial pottery in Mexico centers chiefly in five districts—Guadalajara, Guanajuato, Mexico City, Puebla and Oaxaca. Most of the potters are men who work in dim, damp huts ranged along a patio, several in each hut. In one such house I met a man and his five sons. He was the master potter, and all the boys were at various stages of apprenticeship except one. He wanted to be a lawyer, and the father moaned over his wheel as he confided his fears.

All is very quiet in these little sheds. The potters work intently, seriously, for they are paid by the piece, and every moment is precious. The only sound is the shuffle, shuffle, shuffle of bare feet on wheel, for huaraches are neatly set under each man's table, to be put on at the end of the day. Each worker has rigged up a comfortable seat for himself. Usually they are no more than bare boards suspended on rope, but they seem to give perfect satisfaction.

In the patio outside, men walk around and around great stone jars filled with pigment. They push before them a barked limb of a tree which in turn is attached to a grinding stone by an intricate system of ropes and belts. It works perfectly. Once I saw suspended from the wheel above, an airplane made of gaudy-colored paper—a gay note!

In surroundings such as these are made the dishes and kitchenware and mugs. They come in various shades of ocher, and the boys and women who decorate them draw simple lines in white and green, flowers, animals, a verse, a name, a word of endearment. Five or six processes are usually necessary to complete the article: first, sifting the sand; second, preparing the clay, which is kneaded on a metate, sometimes by women but more usually by the feet of small boys and men. The third process is the molding. Practically all is done by hand; even the larger pieces for which molds are used are generally shaped by hand in the finishing. After molding, the pieces are dried, first in the shade, then in the sun, for several days. If they are not to be glazed, they are decorated immediately after drying; if glazed, they go through one slight baking, then are decorated and sometimes go back for a second baking. The glaze is a wash composed of tin, lead and fine sand, and small boys squat in the patios of the pottery factories and dip the vases and plates in large vats hollowed out of solid stone and filled with this mixture.

The finest quality of commercial pottery made in Mexico comes from Puebla—the "city of the angels"— a three-hour motor ride around the mountain from Mexico City. Here the Indians were at work before the coming of the Spaniards.

When the padres arrived in these cities in the valley of Puebla, they marveled at the manual dexterity of the Indian and immediately wrote home about it, asking that Brothers who knew the art of the potter be sent out to instruct the Indians. As early as the sixteenth century true stanniferous faïence was made in Mexico, though its rediscovery by America did not occur until about 1905, when an old Indian woman was found selling it on the streets of Puebla.

After the coming of the padres, several influences stamped themselves on the work of the Indians. At first the designs of Talavera were copied in lovely whites and deep gray-blues. Then the introduction of Chinese porcelains in Mexico was reflected in Oriental decorations. This was followed by a polychrome period in the later half of the eighteenth century, and then came the gaudy, flamboyant, vulgarized, over-decorated ware still current.

By 1654 the majolica industry in Puebla had grown to such an extent that a potters' guild was established. Laws were made regulating the preparation of the clays and glazes, the different grades, character of decoration, even the sizes of household utensils and the sale of the wares. The makers were required to place on each piece the initials or monogram of the maker, and penalties were provided for the counterfeiting or falsification of trade-marks. The guild continued to flourish until 1676. Then it declined, and its provisions were no longer enforced.

The rules set down by the potters' guild afford much interesting information on the materials and processes used during the seventeenth century as well as today. The glaze for fine pottery was made of one part tin to four and one fourth parts of lead. For the common wares the glaze contained twelve and one half parts lead to one part of tin. At an early date two kinds of clays were employed, white and red. The white clay is softer than the red. When baked slightly, the white clay appears porous and can be easily cut with a knife. But when fired for a longer time it becomes partially vitrified and much harder. Now these clays are combined, and modern potters declare the results to be more satisfactory.

It is only in recent years that the beauty of Puebla majolica has been rightly appreciated. Now there are several excellent collections. One is owned by Señor Bello of Puebla, the other is in the Pennsylvania Museum of Art in Philadelphia, and not so long ago Mrs. Robert Wade de Forest presented her collection, particularly rich in the polychrome variety of pottery, to the Metropolitan Museum in New York City.

If you visit Puebla, step for a few moments into the lovely Chapel of the Rosary. Look around at the dado of this chapel. It is of magnificent ribboned tile. For the monks who encouraged this art in the new colony used a great deal of tile in building. They erected whole churches of it. They crowned the domes of their cathedrals in yellow tiles that greet the morning sun all over the valley of Mexico as brilliantly as the clear crow of the chanticleer.

While the factories in Puebla have gone quite tourist today, you can have lovely things made to order. At the present rate of exchange, the tile made to your own design for an eight by ten bathroom, walls, floor completely covered, will cost you about twenty-eight dollars in American money, at three and one half pesos to a dollar. The last time I visited Mexico I brought home a tiled bathroom, much to the amazement of the customs officer who surveyed my declaration.

If you visit Guadalajara to see the sunsets, visit the little dusty town of Tonala, just beyond, to see the pottery. Some of the loveliest pottery in Mexico comes from there. It is unglazed. Its color is soft gray and reddish-brown decorated with stylized flower and animal motifs, oftentimes painted on with a dog's tail dipped in white and blue pigments. Unfortunately the products of this district have been much influenced by the bad taste of tourists and of American shop buyers. They are now making in great quantities a bluish-gray ware overly ornamented with paintings of burros, cacti and sleeping Indians. Horrible ash trays made like sombreros are also produced here in great quantities, and the demand for them by tourists never seems to be satiated. But here also work such artists as the Galvan brothers, Zacarias Jimon and Ladislao Ortega. The shapes of the pottery produced by the two latter artists are often different from those found in any other parts of Mexico. Frequently they are taller, more graceful and truly classical in their restraint.

The forms preferred by the Galvans are low and bulbous, which is the shape common to the Plateau. The decorations of this pottery consist of stylized flowers, trees and animals, applied with such fine skill and taste as to seem fused with the pottery itself.

The work of Jimon approaches more nearly the vertical shape preferred by the Greeks. That is, the object is tall and slender rather than low and broad. Some of his loveliest work is seen in water jugs, bottles, vases and pitchers.

The work of Ortega leans still further toward the classical. The shapes are finely formed and proud, the decorations restrained, and he frequently departs from the typical flower, bird and animal motifs to adorn his pottery with frets and arabesques such as are seen on the walls of Mitla and the temples of the Greeks, though it is certain that he never saw either of them.

The pottery of these artists and of others who work in the towns about Guadalajara is decorative rather than practical, though when carefully shellacked inside, they become charming flower containers.

Of all the quantities of pottery produced in Mexico, there are three types which are practical and beautiful. These are the dishes made in Oaxaca with a flowing pansy pattern in brown, yellow and blue, highly colorful, fairly durable. Then there is an oatmeal-colored glazed ware from Puebla with charming deep-blue design of bands, the center carrying the painting of a single swan or a deer; this is the strongest ware made in Mexico. And finally there is the kitchenware made for cooking or for the use of the peon, a yellow-red unglazed ware, simply but imaginatively decorated with drawings of birds, animals, leaves, bands and geometric motifs. The quality and durability of this ware is indicated by its "ring." It is fascinating to see the shopper spend hours testing the jugs and pots and mugs in San Juan market, Mexico, until they come upon one that answers satisfactorily.

One of my favorite types of pottery comes from Guerrero. I always use a little pot which I got there to hold my pencils when I write. This pottery is unglazed. It has a soft cream-colored background; it is painted with black-brown lines depicting small flowers and charming little birds. The shapes are beautiful. They usually have three legs and appear decidedly Persian in feeling.

Then there is the seasonal pottery which is to be found only around the days preceding the Day of the Dead. In Oaxaca it is the custom to eat at this feast a thin pancake fried crisp in lard and covered with sweet sirup, then to break your plate. At this time, too, appear beautiful can-

157

dlesticks and censers. One of the most charming of these pieces I saw in the home of Frances Toor. It is a three-legged little pot a foot high. All around the edge are Little Souls with arms upraised as if to praise the good food their descendant has thoughtfully placed in the pot for them to return and eat.

On these occasions and every day in the year the puestras (open-air shops.) are filled with clay figures and toys that delight all children and those who are older. Mrs. Morrow in her delightful book, *The Painted Pig,* has achieved immortality for those little beasts whose fragility and lovableness is at once the delight and the sorrow of the children.

For the toys of Mexico have an ingratiating crudity that is quite irresistible. They have a way of finding a place in your heart entirely out of proportion to their value and quality. Why? No one can explain, but to understand, just shop for them, and you will find yourself buying one to keep no matter how many birthdays may have passed since your toytime days.

Just as travellers in New England find interest and amusement in "collecting" epitaphs from old gravestones so habitués of Mexican markets collect the sayings drawn on pottery by the maker. These messages are sometimes gay, loving, passionate, often sad, occasionally amusing, and have been known to be suggestive to American minds. Here are a few collected by René d'Harnoncourt:

*Light of my eyes, ever beloved Lolita, God bless
you, but do leave me in peace.*

> *The hands that made me*
> *Would caress you*
> *As they touched me*
> *When they made me.*
> *Juan Gomez made me.*

And from a pitcher for pulque:

> *Pulque from the Sierras Matas*
> *Makes me stagger on my journey,*
> *Throws me down and ends my life—*
> *That's all.*

CHAPTER ELEVEN

Weavings for Use and for Sale

JUST when the Indians of Mexico began to weave was a debatable question until 1928. In that year well-preserved samples of woven cotton goods were discovered in a cave. The pottery in the cave indicated that the cloth dated from the time of the Old Empire, about the fifth century.

When the Spaniards arrived, they found that the Aztecs, Otomis and Tarascans were expert weavers, working in fibers, cotton and feathers. Today this art is practically unchanged in methods and craftsmanship. Cotton, henequen and maguey fibers are still used, and to these have been added wool, the gift of the conquistadors. But the art of weaving is no longer what it was!

One afternoon I visited the home of a friend who is an enthusiastic collector of old textiles. He had prepared for my visit by summoning two Indian boys. They were to be the "mannequins." And for several hours these lads did nothing but unfold before our eyes sheets from Toluca, eighteenth-century zerapes from Saltillo, rebozos, sashes, tilnas, huipils, ayates. The glory of the colors, the beauty of the rich designs made me think that I had become lost in the court of some East Indian maharajah. As the light fell upon these wondrous old textiles, they glowed with all the rich fire of polished jewels. My eyes became dazed with their colors, soft, rich, warm, exotic. The room became alive with color; the very air seemed permeated with it. I felt as if I were actually living in a stained glass window or in a giant mosaic. Constantly repeating itself was the remembrance of the crude way in which these beautiful textiles came into being, but this thought only served to enhance the wonder of it all.

It was not until the Spaniards came that the Indian knew the horizontal loom. Today you will find horizontal looms set up in little huts, usually in pairs. The Indian of Mexico is ever gregarious and does not wish to work alone. Oftentimes the loom is nothing more than the rough-barked limbs of trees. On these upright looms most of the weaving is done by men. The women cling to the preconquest loom, called telar de abate, which is merely a couple of twigs fastened to a post or tree and tied by a band around the waist of the weaver. The weft is beaten down by a wooden sword, and the women have a clever way of bracing themselves to avoid the thump—important since they are usually pregnant. When the design is complicated, a number of heddles are used.

A wheel is used for spinning, usually the work of the women. The preconquest distaff is called the malacate and is made of pottery. It is small, round, with ornamental designs modeled in the heavy clay. It is fitted into a stick or a bobbin and "danced" in a bowl. I also saw the spinning wheel such as was used in colonial America. In fact, I spent a very pleasant lunch time sharing my sandwiches and drinking my Teohuacan water with a beautiful Indian woman and her six-year-old daughter. While I dawdled in the shade, they never stopped work. The woman spun, and the little girl continued her carding, using two wooden paddles nearly as big as she was with wire prongs along which she dragged the wool.

The baby, two years old, slept on the ground, completely covered by a zerape that was so beautiful in color and design that I longed to own it, but their hospitality could not be insulted by the suggestion of a sale. When I hopefully commented on the baby's covering, the mother glanced casually toward it and said, "It is for use," then nodded toward the hut in the rear of the cactus-walled patio and told me that there were zerapes made for sale.

I had come to Teotilan del Valle, the village of the weavers, from Oaxaca, the nearest city. As I jogged over the loose gravel road, I decided to visit the Temple of Mitla before calling on the weavers at Teotilan, as I wished to spend much time with them.

162

Mitla is the corruption of an Aztecan word meaning "place of the dead." It is the site of a burial ground and the temple of the same name is in a sun-flooded valley where the Zapotecs found a generous supply of easily-worked stone, at once tractable and durable. To the craftsman who must work with stone and obsidian, knowing neither metal tools nor the wheel, this stone was far more advantageous than the flinty quartzite of Monte Alban or the basaltic lava of Teotihuacan.

There are no pyramids at Mitla. The temples rest on low platforms of rubble and are only one story high. The roofs are no more, but the walls are masterpieces of American aboriginal art. Their surface consists of mosaics of separately carved stones in geometrical designs, fitted together without mortar. The walls are about four feet thick, and there are 150 panels of these mosaics running continuously along the walls of four great chambers. The corners of these walls are huge flat stones, so perfectly fitted without cement that "they appear like tables brought together."

The mosaics are not painted. To color them would be to gild the lily. But every tone of light and shade plays on them while the sun flows down from the cloudless sky above. The clear silver light of early morning, gentle, persuasive; the relentless, deeply-etching light of the midday tropical sun; the luminous rose rays of the setting sun; each picks out the glory of those mosaics, creating an hourly panorama of ever-changing beauty that rivals the magnificence of the skies. Mitla by moonlight!

163

Mitla under the pure white rays of that silver crescent that only these tropical lands know—that is a sight I hope I may see once more before I pass!

But there are more wonders here than these arabesques. Strange cruciform tombs lined with a red stucco of greater strength than has ever yet been produced anywhere. Massive tensile stones weighing from ten to fifteen tons. On some of these the cathedral, which the padres always loved to erect over places of pagan worship, sprawls its mediocre breadth over the plain. In an open court are columns standing upright, defying the centuries regardless of the despoliation of the elements and the rigors of frequent earthquakes which so often shake this volcanic land. But always one returns to the wonder of the mosaics. There are not more than a half dozen motifs, only one of which has a curved line, but the effect is never monotonous; they are woven over the walls like a theme through the variations of a symphony. In them light and shadow are transformed to stone. The unknown Indians who conceived and wrought this art took on the very majesty of the God who said, "Let there be light." For light, the challenge, the benediction, the very source of all art, finds reason for its being in the mosaics of Mitla, the place of the dead. Mitla is pure beauty in sculpture, as the Bach theme on the G string is pure beauty in music.

Imagine the labor that went into these arabesques! The hours, weeks and years spent rubbing stone against stone until their very textures were fused. The wonder of the construction of Mitla is the fact that without symmetry a harmonious beauty has been created. The lines of the mosaics are not parallel upon measurement, but to the eye they are perfect. Of all the world's *trompes d'oeil,* Mitla is supreme.

But these arts of architecture and of sculpture are no more. Only on the far southern reaches of this plateau did they ever flower, at Chichen Itza in Yucatan, at Copan, while the authority, Verrill, declares that the temple of Palenque in Chiapas, a couple of hundred miles to the south, "is perhaps the finest example of prehistoric architecture in the entire world." All these wonders were created long ago. When Europe was in the depths of the Dark Ages, the culture of America was at its zenith. To-day the Indian, conquered, but born to victory, works on with whatever materials he has at hand, creating beauty from the earth with timeless patience, intelligent concentration, with a mind rich in tradition and imagination and with bronze hands dexterous and prolific.

One of the most productive villages of weavers in Mexico is Teotilan del Valle, which lies near the village of Mitla, dusty, quiet, basking in the sun. Each little patio is fenced with twelve-foot spires of organ cactus, and one enters through a narrow break in the fierce fence into a courtyard where pigs and chickens search for food and into a second patio where the wife spins, the children card, and the littlest baby sleeps. In a hut in the third courtyard, two crude looms are set up, mute testimony of the Indian's invariable communism.

I was in the hut scarcely a moment when company began to arrive, little brown men with great sombreros and zerapes piled on their shoulders. Each one came up to shake hands solemnly with our host. They waited patiently while I questioned him about the crude paper silhouettes of Aztec gods hanging on nails on the wall.

"I copied them from the Caso's book," the weaver proudly said. His eyes were quick with intelligence. He started to weave, his nimble bronze fingers sending the gay-colored balls of yarn back and forth with incredible speed.

Finally, my attention was diverted by the company now becoming a crowd in the little room. They were quick to catch my interest.

"Mire—mire," one whispered, pointing to an adjoining hut. I went in. The long, low room was amazingly cool after the heat of the noonday sun. There was nothing in the hut but some neatly rolled petates at one end and at the other, an altar with little shrines in which gaudy statues of the Virgin, St. Anthony and the Crucifixion were surrounded with paper roses, some pots of flowers and bowls of eggs. In a moment the room was filled with little brown men.

"Mire, patroncita."

"Mire, señorita."

Then I would hold up the zerapes, like hammocks, with

first one little brown man and then another. Finally my preference came down to two, and we closed the deal.

Each craft center produces a zerape typical of the village. Those woven in Teotilan del Valle have soft white and gray-striped borders, some with a large red or gray center with a stylized lion carrying a rose on his back. For the tourists in American shops they produce stripe-bordered zerapes with idols in the center, and horrible calendar-stones and fierce eagles of vivid color. They told me that they can make all their own colors with herbs and vegetables except red, which always runs. Their orange, yellow, blue are of vegetable origin and beautiful in tone. Green is a source of much trouble to the weavers —they make it themselves and also buy it.

In Xacatapen, Jalisco, the zerapes are heavy and soft, with dark, natural wool colors, beautiful borders and centers of bright flowers. From Sonora come coarse heavy zerapes of distinguished texture and design. Sometimes the designs are ornate and appear in border and center. From San Luis Potosi come the light, striped zerapes adored by the dashing Charros, who wear them on parade in Mexico City on Sunday. Saltillo, once a great craft center, now produces gaudy-striped zerapes that mark the lowest decline of a once great art.

Antique zerapes are still for sale in a few shops in Mexico City, such as Sanborn's. They are glorious in color, soft as satin in texture, and their patterns have a simple, economical distinction. The evenness of their weave is truly marvelous. They are becoming

167

scarcer every day, and consequently their price is mounting. Even with the favorable Mexican exchange a good antique zerape (that is, one about two hundred years old) will be priced from three hundred to a thousand American dollars.

Modern zerapes can be bought in all the curio shops, the markets and in the villages of the weavers, even off the Indians' backs. And it is interesting to note that the Indians themselves never wear the gaudy multi-colored eagle-and-snake-decorated zerapes that have such a lamentable fascination for the tourist.

Practically the same attributes which characterize good Navaho weavings hold true for zerapes. They are to be chosen for the evenness and firmness of their weave, beauty of pattern and the softness and richness of their colorings. Despite the extensive use of aniline dyes, it is still possible to get beautiful zerapes colored with vegetable dyes in soft shades of rose, blue, yellow, green, and purple. The brown wool is usually a natural color, as is the soft creamy-white shade. Weight is also to be considered when making your selection, as it denotes the amount of wool in the piece, its durability and also the firmness of its weave. If you want to go so far as to check up on the market value of wool you can find it listed on the business pages of metropolitan newspapers. Compare it with the weight of your zerape, and more often than not you will find that the difference leaves pitifully little for the arduous work of weaving.

Zerapes are priced according to weight, the fineness

and evenness of the weaving, and if an unusually beautiful piece comes off the loom, the Indian may price it a trifle higher. But usually zerapes are priced like silver, according to weight. The important matters of design and coloring are up to you. In the better shops the poorest ones have been weeded out before you see them, and in this way you are protected not only from a poor buy but also from the adventure of discovering a beauty among the horde. If you do bargain a zerape off an Indian's back, take it to a laundry quickly, have it scoured and boiled. This is the only sure cure for fleas which I have discovered. These pests are perpetually prevalent in the warmer zones and delight in such soft, warm beds.

Zerapes are easy to pack, which is an added incentive to purchase them, and they can be of practical use in the home. Just sew up the center through which the Indian puts his head, and you have a sturdy couch throw or spread. The lighter ones make warm coverlets. The smaller zerapes make excellent rugs for dens, bathrooms, hallways and bedrooms. They fit into the modern interior or the peasant room admirably, and their rich colors and bold designs mate well with sturdy maple and pine furniture. As wall hangings and even as portières they give splendid service, and youngsters adore them for play clothes because they are warm and do not bind active arms and legs.

What the zerape is to the man, the rebozo is to the woman. The rebozo is probably the rebirth of the Moorish shawl and was introduced by the Spaniards, but now every Indian woman and every girl child of not more than six has one. For in Mexico and Guatemala the little ones dress exactly like their elders, grown-ups in miniature.

The rebozo is worn around the shoulders for warmth. It is twisted about the head in a thousand ways as a protection from the sun and as a covering for the head in church. It makes a cradle for the baby while it suckles or while the mother works or while both acts occur simultaneously. Rebozos are just strips of cloth half a yard wide and three yards long, but the women have a thousand ways of draping them—all with a grace and a purposefulness that come only with centuries of use. You can buy the most beautiful rebozo in Mexico, but you can never win from it the grace which an Indian woman gets out of the poorest strip of cotton and rayon.

The decline of the rebozo is one of the misfortunes of these people. In years gone by they were woven of cotton. Laws governed their color. The peon could wear only brown and white or blue and white or dark green and white. But they evaded this law by weaving in them threads of silver and of gold, and so fine was their workmanship that these old rebozos can be drawn through a ring—and not a large one at that.

Today the rebozo of the poor holds to dark blue, green or gray. It is of striped or stylized design, woven of cotton and rayon. The more prosperous sometimes have silk rebozos in garish greens, yellow-reds. But they are both more costly and uglier than the simpler ones woven of cotton and rayon.

The one article of clothing that seems to have suffered least of all is the sash, worn mostly by the women, but also by the men. This is made of both wool and cotton and varies from an inch and a half in width to a half dozen inches and is from one to three yards long.

Every little girl strings up a loom under a shady tree and begins to weave her sash when she is no more than eight years old. Because these sashes have retained their identity it has been my joy to collect them. Three of the loveliest ones I have were bought from three Otomi Indian women who boarded a train on which I was riding. They wore the great, full homespun skirts, miraculously pleated and held in place with a narrow sash woven of fine cotton thread in a distinguished series of intricate designs.

We had great fun and much difficulty effecting the sale as the train lurched along. Changing their sashes for men's belts which I had intended for gifts brought forth gales of laughter, but I had the satisfaction of knowing that they had more pesos and I had three museum pieces. But what must they think of the foolish American!

Have you ever seen a dealer who hadn't a weakness? Sooner or later they become impregnated with their own germ and fall. My weakness is ayates.

Mexico is a land of contrasts. Airplanes carrying mail

cast down their shadows on little brown men and women trotting along the road bearing flowers, food, pottery, furniture, baskets, in the carrying cloths that they have used since the days of Montezuma. The weight which these little brown people can carry for hours on end up and down mountain roads is one of the puzzles of this constantly amazing land. Into these cloths they crowd these incredible weights and let them hang from their foreheads. They call these cloths ayates.

The ayate among the Otomi Indians in the state of Mexico is really a marriage garment. When a young couple state their determination to marry, work begins. The bride's family makes one half of the ayate, a strip about three fourths of a yard wide, about one and one half yards long, and the groom's family makes the other half. The ceremony consists of sewing together the two halves.

When the groom comes to claim his bride, he bears his part of the ayate filled with fruit, sweets and flowers for the wedding feast. When the couple go to their home, they carry their presents in it. But this is not the end of that ayate's usefulness, for it then begins its practical life as a carrying cloth. Thereafter, the man may carry his tools or the woman her baby in it. It may serve as a wrap for a cool morning or for carrying candles when they go on their annual pilgrimage to the Shrine of the Señor de Chalma.

Ayates are difficult to obtain because of the sentiment attached to them. Old ones made with vegetable dyes are very rare. Some are finely woven of cotton, others are coarsely made of the maguey fiber, some are richly embroidered and are used as cloths on the altars which are set up in every home. Riding along the roads, you may see a woman carrying her baby in an ayate which hangs from her forehead; meanwhile spinning the fiber for another as she walks to market. For those nimble fingers never seem to cease working. You may watch the Indian in the market gossiping, bartering, and all the while her quick fingers will be weaving straw of such fineness that your eyes cannot follow it. She never looks at it. Those sensitive fingers weave on and on with never a false move. Never were hands more wondrous than in Mexico!

While the ayate has a sentimental significance, nothing is quite so close to the people as the petate. The materials used, the method of making these reed and palm mats remain to this day exactly as they were in the time of the Aztecs.

In Mexico the Indian comes into this world on a petate and goes out of it rolled in a petate. As a child he plays on it, and when he grows up he eats on it, prays on it, sleeps on it. His wedding gifts are placed on it; the dishes given to the beloved dead on the Day of the Dead, November 2, are placed on a petate. It becomes the floors and walls of his house. So it is not surprising that the petate has become a figure of speech in the language. To indicate that a person is not of the same rank as oneself is to say, "Those fleas do not jump on my petate."

To indicate inconsistency and irresponsibility is to say, "A petate flame." To indicate vulgarity is to say, "He who is born on a petate will always belch reeds." And death is announced by the phrase, "He has tied up his petate."

The petate is woven by hand wherever reeds are grown in Mexico, and that is practically everywhere. The reeds are cut, dried and then woven in several motifs, all of which are coarse, except in Puebla, where they make a fine palm petate and decorate it with geometrical motifs in reds, blues, yellows and violet. This type is also produced in Oaxaca. In the villages near Mexico City this same material also serves to create the most delightful toys—fierce generals on horseback, houses, boats, wagons, even figures of Christ and His angels.

These reed rugs make cool-looking effective floor coverings for summer homes. Their cheapness invites purchase, but their fragility makes the chore of shipping them home hardly worth while. The children adore petate toys because their lightness makes them easy to lug about and their toughness withstands the hazards of play.

PART THREE

THE TEXTILES OF GUATEMALA

CHAPTER TWELVE

Altitude and Finery

THE flight from Mexico to Guatemala City is made in an afternoon. By train, it is three long torturous days of heat, dust and delay until one reaches the capital, Guatemala City, which is the focus from which many good roads branch out into the mountains. If one wishes to know the textiles for which this country is famous, one leaves the city for the drive over the mountains to beautiful Lake Atitlan, a giant sapphire walled by the great volcanoes, San Pedro, Toleman and Atitlan, then on to Las Encuentoas—which is nine thousand feet above sea level. Thence to Chichicastenango or Quezaltenango and Totanicapan.

There are about two hundred and seventy-five distinct

177

costumes in Guatemala, but now that the products of machinery are making such inroads in the land, it is growing more and more difficult to see the beautiful costumes that the Indians have worn uninterruptedly since before the days of the conquest. However, even on a short trip one can easily become familiar with a couple of dozen different types.

For the roads are peopled with Indians carrying their wares to market. Burros never seem to have come south of the Mexican border. All transportation of merchandise is done on man-back and woman-back. As you motor along over the roads that perpetually ascend the heights and descend into the barrancas, in a few days' travel you can learn to recognize the men from Solala with short checked skirts fastened in the rear, the women from Santiago Atitlan with their skirts wrapped so tightly around their hips and thighs that you wonder that they can move, the Maxenos men with their short black jackets and small clothes and the Maxenos women in heavily decorated huipils.

The Guatematicos, which are of the Quiche tribe of Indians, are reserved and dignified. Even when in their cups they are never aroused to the amorous buoyance of their neighbors, the Indians of Mexico, but become even more stolid, morose, and world-weary. The years of their old race seem to rest upon them. As servants they are gentle, quiet, submissive, and the children are more respectful, less confiding. They cross their arms, bow their heads, and wait for your finger to touch them before raising their lovely little faces.

In Guatemala the men not only wear costumes as colorful and fantastic as the women's but actually make them themselves. It is a fair challenge to bet whether in the course of a day or two you will see more amazing head-dresses on the women or more astounding millinery on the men. For the Beau Brummells of Los Altos are seldom content with one hat but wear two simultaneously. Nor are they consistent in their choice of materials. It is quite possible to see a felt hat worn between two straw ones, the combination achieving an amazing minaret effect more incongruous than the domes of the Kremlin.

Every village has its special costume, but the vast majority of Indians do not live in the city but in the highlands where they can find an area of land with sufficient water to raise the essential corn and a few pigs and chickens. Those who live in the tierra caliente and work on the coffee fincas and banana plantations have adopted the drab calzones, more or less ragged and dirty.

Legend says that it was the third Toltec emperor, Hunahper, who reigned in Yucatan, who was first to show the Quiches the wonders of cotton. Wool was of course introduced by the Spaniards. Silk began to be imported when Chinese trade was developed in the eighteenth and nineteenth centuries. These fibers are worked and dyed by hand, but gradually this custom is passing. Thread factories are now established in Guatemala, and this machine-made product, together with rayon and aniline dyes, is winning the weavers more and more away from the fine quality of the old handmade textiles. However, it is still possible to visit the weavers in their homes and watch the preparation of cotton going on as it was before a certain ruthless, ambitious, victorious, Alvarado conquered the country with four hundred and fifty Spaniards and a retinue of Indians.

Cotton, both white and brown, grows extensively on the middle plateaus, and now sheep graze in the higher altitudes. To prepare the cotton, a cushion is made of cornhusks covered with deerskin. On this the cotton is beaten with two sticks that make a pleasant rhythmic sound. When fluffed in this way, it is ready for the spindle.

This is a stick pointed on one end and cut about eighteen inches long. About four or five inches from one end is a whorl made of clay or wood. Women squat on the ground and turn this spindle in a wooden bowl with one hand and feed the cotton with the other. After the cotton is fed from the spindle to a revolving reed, it is then ready for the winding frame. This may be nothing more or less than a long, crude board raised on sticks a few inches from the ground. It is interesting to note that invariably women prepare the cotton and men prepare the wool.

The looms are most primitive. Men use rapid foot looms, while a woman will pick up a couple of fairly smooth sticks, tie them to a handy tree or post and, squatting on the earth, weave a bit of textile that we, with all our skill and fine machines, cannot duplicate.

Some of the textiles have a padded appearance; others are ribbonlike. Some have a drawn-work weave that seems impossible to produce on a loom. Invariably the weaving is even, beautiful in design and rich in color, and one of the tests of the worthiness of a wife is her ability to weave. Consequently little girls begin to weave soon after they learn to walk, the better to get a husband.

No less amazing than the weaving itself is the dyeing. European civilization may have mastered metals, but for centuries these Indians have studied the fibers, barks, grasses, insects, even the fish, and from them have wrought colors an artist in stained glass might well envy.

I have an aboriginal fondness for purple, so I will mention this color first because to me it is the most beautiful of all. Guatematicos use on their ceremonial garments a rich, soft purple made from mollusks. The men gather them. It is said that the fish live only seven years and that it is best to gather them in the spring when the moon is full.

The men go down to the streams, rub one animal against the other, and in this way a saliva is extracted from a gland in the gill. Strands of wool are dipped into the excretion, and this dye renders a magnificent purple which gives the garment a peculiar seaweed odor and a salty taste. The mollusk is then returned to the water and not annoyed until the next season.

The rich blue dyes seen in skirts and in the embroidery

on blouses come from the leaves of the sacatenta plant, for indigo is no longer cultivated. The nance fruit supplies brown. When a very deep shade is desired, the bark of the aliso tree is employed. The bright yellow is obtained from the excrement of certain birds, while green comes from the taray and orange color from an almond. The little insect cochineal, which propagates on the underleaves of the maguey, provides the rich, clear red.

Two methods of dyeing are used. There is the usual dip way and a remarkable tie-and-dye process in which each fine cotton strand is counted. The result is a marvelous *jaspé* effect. For setting the color, a liquid made by mashing the leaves of the tempate is used. This tree grows profusely all over Guatemala.

When wool is the material to be colored, cochineal is used for red, as in cotton, but when blue is desired, the material is put in a solution of bichromate of potash with the bark of the campeachy tree. Before wool is dyed brown it is boiled for a long time in lime water and then dipped in the liquid extracted from the aliso tree, while green comes from bark of the palo amarello tree.

In the highlands the woman's dress consists of a huipil, or blouse; a refojas, or skirt; a belt; a cinta, or headribbon; and a servilletas, or carrying cloth. In some sections the skirt worn above the knee indicates that its wearer is a maiden; when it comes below the knee, that she is a married woman. However, the very full skirts worn in other districts do not have this significance, and they almost always come to the ankle. No shoes are worn, and the degree of wealth is indicated by necklaces of old silver coins and coral, now unfortunately being discarded for garish glass beads from Czecho-Slovakia.

The most showy article produced by the Guatemalans is the huipil (pronounced wee-pill), or blouse, worn by the women. This varies from the short blouse which reveals a lovely strip of brown stomach (as in Palin) to the long, flowing blouses that fall to the knees. Others still are tucked within the skirt to become a petticoat.

Cotton is the material most often used in making huipils. The textures range from the very lightweight ones worn in the warmer altitudes, some of which are almost transparent, to exceedingly heavy ones worn in Los Altos. Multicolored stripes are a popular design. For instance, on a brown cotton there will be woven a broad red stripe, with narrow bands of red and a pin-line of yellow; a huipil of white cotton will have stripes of indigo-blue and red; others will combine yellow and purple and a cream-colored ground or black and red on a deep ivory shade. Some huipils are of a natural-colored homespun, wondrously embroidered in red, blue and purple; still others combine both woven stripes and embroidered motifs in the blaze of color characteristic of medieval stained glass. However varied, rich, glowing their colors may be, the effect is never garish.

The huipils all vary in width, but usually consist of two or three sections sewn together according to the custom of the community. In Quezaltenango a plain satin stitch is used, or a gaily-colored chain stitch with flowered design, while in Villaneuve the sections are held together by loose stitches with plain cotton thread, reminding one of the bride who said she sewed her trousseau "with long and loving stitches."

The necklines are finished in many charming ways, some as ornate as a bead necklace. Sometimes a buttonhole stitch and insets of store-bought ribbon or braid or a decorative herringbone stitch is used. And then, of course, all huipils have their special purpose. There is the everyday one, the one for church, for maternity, and the wedding huipil. The latter is usually woven by the girl's godmother, or madrina, as she is called.

Two kinds of skirts are woven. The "envelope," which is five or six yards wide, and the plegodas, which are eight yards wide. Some are worn to the knee, others to the ankle, and some are wrapped about the hips so tightly that movement seems impossible. All are arranged and held in place with belts. To see a woman drape these yards and yards of fabric with every fold perfectly in place, with only the aid of a belt is truly amazing!

The belts themselves are wondrous examples of weaving. Some are less than two inches wide; others are so wide as almost to serve as a garment. Elaborate fringe and tassels decorate some, while maternity belts have two small pieces of obsidian sewed on them. This is to prevent the passage of the baby to another enceinte woman should one meet her on the road.

But the pride of the woman of Guatemala is her elaborate headdress. It is beautifully woven of cotton, wool and perhaps silk. When narrow, it is braided into the hair and plaited around the head. Large strands of wool in black, red, and purple are also woven through the braids and piled high like huge, bulbous turbans. Some of the ceremonial turbans are very wide, with enormous tassels seven yards long falling over the head like a veil. The women of Santa Maria Chiquimila twist their hair into mounds with strips of red cloth and then tuck into this headdress all the hair that falls during combing, as it is considered bad luck to throw away one's hair.

Servelletas, or carrying cloths, are used by both men and women. These are decorated with colorful tribal designs, usually on white backgrounds, and sometimes are richly fringed. They have a myriad of uses: to cover food, to cradle the baby, to pad the top of the head when carrying a heavy load, to serve as a head bandana. The ceremonial carrying cloths are used to hold the staff of office during a parade or to anchor a statue on its bier during a religious procession. All of which will lead you to conclude, and rightly, that the Guatemalan belle is a much dressed-up lady. And the men are not less so!

The costume of the men consists of a shirt, a jacket, trousers, a belt of leather or of woven cotton. Many of the costumes are obviously copied from those worn by the courtiers of sixteenth- and seventeenth-century Spain.

The coats, often short and bolero-like, are trimmed with braid and are valued for the number of their pockets. In the highlands, these coats are made of a closely woven, almost stiff material; farther down the plateau one finds homespun cotton coats, gaily lined and embroidered back and front with charming little beast and bird designs worked in colored silks.

Flour bags are a popular fabric for trousers, and the more flaming the trade-mark, the better the Indian likes it. In the market you will see Indians spend half a day turning over the bags to make sure that the most glowing trade-mark is secured. Sometimes two pairs of trousers are worn. The top trousers are split, and the under ones boast of embroidery which flutters out at the sides.

I have already spoken of the amazing millinery fashions in vogue among the men, but they also wear turbans, bandanas and caps that are beautiful and becoming. Also popular is a palm-leaf hat which they weave for themselves. Bags in endless variety are woven and used by the men but their trumplines are their most prized possessions. Men in Guatemala never use baskets. Instead, they carry all their loads with the aid of a trumpline, which is a length of oxhide, the hairy side worn next to the forehead. It is interesting to watch them assemble a load. It is done with all the amazing orderliness and neatness characteristic of the Indian. He builds up, he tests, he maneuvers. Finally all is fixed to his satisfaction, and with a hundred-pound load or more suspended from his head, he is off for a ten-mile trot to market and back.

And in Guatemala once again we meet the question, "What do Indian designs mean?"

The majority of authorities on the textiles produced in every other part of this plateau are agreed that Indian designs have no religious or tribal significance. The motifs are merely conventionalized copies of sun, tree, bird, flower, delineated in the simple geometric lines of which the Indian is capable. This belief is not stated in a disparaging manner. Those familiar with Indian art are deeply appreciative of the culture which is capable of integrating utility, beauty and religious thought in articles made for everyday use. The Indian mind, like that of the Oriental, is orderly. You have only to witness the perfect regularity of their social customs, the arrangement of town and pueblo, the neatness with which even a handful of beans or peanuts or eggs is stacked in their orderly markets to recognize this remarkable characteristic. So it is not surprising that the things made with their brown hands come to be decorated and beautified by the force which is the elemental creator of this trait—Nature.

The life of the Indian was always governed by the aspects of nature, by sun, rain, drought, flood. Living close to the earth, he witnessed Nature in her most beneficent and most terrifying moods. He saw spring come and harvest fade into the barrenness of winter. And life in animals was not greatly different from life in plants, except that the life span of the one was longer. Nature,

then, was the motivating force on which the Indian pat-
terned his own life, and he wove or molded her outward
symbols into the things he used. Thus were created vases,
jars, blankets, baskets, equal in form, color and technique
to those of the finest civilizations of Europe and the
Orient. So a noble environment kindled a noble art, and
the true greatness of the plateau primitives is that they
are capable of reflecting in art the beauty of the life about
them.

However, the culture of Guatemala differs from the
Indian cultures of Mexico and the pueblos in that the
Guatemalan designs do have significance. Authorities on
Guatemalan textiles believe this even though today the
weavers themselves may not be aware of the underlying
meanings of the motifs they weave out of their heads.
Probably the story of these symbols was known only to
the ancient priests and shamans, who have died with their
secrets or passed them on only to the few ordained and
educated in the faiths of the ancients.

As you finger huipils, belts, napkins, you find the
curved horseshoe line that might be the plumed serpent,
Quetsatl. You recognize the turkey or peacock known as
Tlaloc, the God of Fertility. You see plants growing out
of a small vessel on which perches a bird which may easily
be the Bird on the Tree of Life. Human figures holding
feathers may have some reference to the ceremonial
feather dances. The designs are never put in with curved
lines but in cross-stitch effects. Sometimes they are woven
so as to puff up above the surface. Sometimes the object

is completely covered. Again, it may be decorated with dramatic economy. In this country you also find the weavers putting their own marks on their works, just as potters and silversmiths have done through the ages, but if a weaving should develop to perfection, the weaver deliberately makes a mistake. Perfection may never be human; it is a quality of the supernaturals.

The significance of colors, however, is still generally appreciated. Black represents the color of weapons, which, in the days of the Maja, were made of obsidian. Yellow symbolizes corn, or food; red is the blood of sacrifice, while blue is the color of royalty.

It is not so much fun to shop in Guatemala as it is in Mexico. For the Guatemalan currency is on a par with that of America, while in Mexico the value of the peso is far below that of the dollar. You notice the difference instantly. But for the lover of textiles, the products of Guatemala seem to cost but a fraction of their real worth regardless of the unfavorable currency. The situation has, however, hindered the shops and stores in America from importing Guatemalan products, since they do not permit the high markup that Mexican wares do. However, one of the finest textiles I have, decorated with the desirable but seldom-to-be-had fertility symbol, I found in a New York department store at a very reasonable price.

The blouses, or huipils, can often be converted into stunning beach costumes and lounging robes. Others can have the neck opening sewn together. They will serve as colorful table throws and luncheon cloths. Very handsome tablecloths can be made by inserting the belts and sashes between lengths of hand-spun linen. They also make effective curtain tiebacks if you can screw up the courage to cut up anything so lovely.

The voluminous homespun skirts are so sturdy and strong that they make excellent upholstery and decorative fabrics, and their colors are so rich that they create a pleasing contrast with the severity of early American maple and pine furniture. But why must you buy them for use? Surely their beauty is a sufficient reason for their being.

When shopping in the market or—and I speak literally—off the Indian's back, see to it that the fabrics are not damaged by use. Beware of highly lustrous threads which indicate the presence of rayon. Choose for the variety and the evenness of the weave and for the softness of their texture, for the beauty of color, the fine designs and the multiplicity of motifs which are so charming.

In the shops of Guatemala City, in the market place at Chichicastenango and Quezaltenango, it is possible to buy these lovely textiles. But if you are going to visit Guatemala your best plan is simply to buy the clothes off the Indians. This takes time, but persistence will win.

CHAPTER THIRTEEN

Moderns of Ancient Ways

THE art of the Indian is doomed. When the first white settler set foot on this continent, its death knell sounded. Now the materialistic and mechanized civilization of the white man is strangling the red man's culture. The Indian must keep pace with the world about him, or pass out of it. His cup is broken. The artistry of a great race is diminishing to nothingness like the coils of its own baskets.

The art span of this unique race has been remarkably productive, though brief. When these people migrated to this plateau no one knows, but here a culture that had nothing in common with the old world was developed. It is supposed that the Indian was of Mongolian origin, and, left alone, who knows but that the descendants of the same yellow horde that developed the rich culture of China might have achieved an equally great culture on this western plateau? Whatever might have been is merely conjecture. The fact remains that here on the spine of this continent a unique and rare culture was developed. Here was produced one of the few really great expressions of beauty that the world has ever known. To understand and to appreciate this art you must know the race in whose brown hands it flowered.

No white man can completely know the red man. The difference in ideology is too great. To all of us who have been privileged to come in contact with him, some few of his complex characteristics are revealed. We see him as if reflected in one of his own obsidian mirrors, but darkly. I, for one, am humbled by the image and realize that I may only interpret it sparsely, no matter how earnestly I may try. What I do not see in these primitive people, another may recognize in bold relief. What seems important to me may be far less appealing to another. Just today I was sitting before the desk of a woman who for thirty years has conducted a business which has made a fortune for her, a good living for many, and which enjoys a rare distinction in industry by reason of its high principles of integrity, persistently pursued.

"Whatever you do, do it well," she said. "Even a trivial thing becomes worth while when it is well done."

Quick as a flash I saw in this modern, cultured professional woman a kinship with the primitive women of the plateau. Their aims were similar, though so widely different, so diversely expressed. To do everything well, no matter how important it might be nor how trivial.

That to me seems to be the fundamental characteristic of the culture of the plateau. The primitive woman working in the shade of her adobe hut or under the shelter of some kindly tree made every bowl, basket or blanket a work of love. Hers was a constant striving for the ideal. Working with only crude tools, with only grasses, clay and wool for materials, she constantly sought to create beauty. Her ideal was not success in terms of dollars but the realization of integrity of soul. Her sophistication was truly genuine; it was her purpose to be unfailingly courteous, unfailingly charming throughout the everyday routine.

There are some who, looking at the primitives of the plateau, wonder at their self-restraint and self-denial, their self-respect and self-sufficiency; others marvel at their endurance, endless patience and gentleness; still others are amazed at their aloofness and their pride, which is so great as to seem humble. The dexterity of their hands is a never-failing source of amazement, as their mental processes are a constant source of despair.

An understanding of these traits can be approached only when you meet the Indian in his own land. He lived in the Almighty's Amphitheater. Around him was the continuous evidence of supernatural power. He knew floods and droughts, earthquakes and volcanoes, rich harvests and relentless famines. Powerless to explain

193

these phenomena, the Indian sought recourse in a belief in supernatural beings. The roll of thunder, the crash of lightning, the ebb and flow of waters, the changing seasons, health, fertility—all were personified. Even the animals who furnished him with food and warmth became gods in his populous pantheon and lived intimately with him. The Indian endowed all supernaturals with human qualities so that they might be approached and their favor won in ways that he, in his simplicity, could understand—with gifts of flowers and food, with ceremonies and sacrifices. Every act, no matter how trivial or important, was performed in communion with the great powers.

The symbols of these supernaturals were the motifs worked into the basket, woven into the blanket, hammered into metal, molded into clay. Therefore, these utilitarian objects came to rise above the commonplace as do the mountains above the desert. An art was born!

So it is not surprising to find that the popular arts of the plateau possess the same characteristics. They are made by hand according to ancient methods. The materials used are of the simplest, most rudimentary sort. Their decorations are geometric, their coloring restrained, though in some instances rich—glowingly so.

Use was the function of these textiles, baskets and pottery, but beauty was their goal. And so fine was the culture of the Indian that they achieved this purpose nobly. Theirs is an art not cold, keen, imperious, like the art of the ancient Egyptians, but vital, sincere, appealing.

It was not an art bound by leisure, by extreme wealth, nor enforced penury, as we Americans know art today. The art of the plateau was a flowering of daily needs— an everyday art. It was the material expression of their prayer "to make all about me beautiful."

It is true that the people of the plateau work in crude fiber, wool and clay and that clay can never attain the splendor of marble; but it can be good clay. And if your taste is authentic you cannot help recognizing beauty in these lower forms, though you may prefer the higher. Bad taste appears only when sincerity is lacking, and true appreciation of beauty is often quite divorced from a desire to possess. Yet I challenge you to live with these jugs for water, baskets for corn, blankets for warmth and not win from them an intimate satisfaction.

Brown hands have made them, and they lack the cloying perfection rendered by the machine. But if true purity were the sole attribute of beauty, music then would consist only of the sounds of a tuning fork. The imperfections are to the basket, pot, or blanket, what dissonance is to music. Just as discord intensifies the satisfaction which follows the resolution of the harmony, so you become actually grateful to the flaws in these lovely forms. What is lost in perfection is gained in appeal.

Indian art stimulates imagination. Thoughts of labor, sun, dust, fatigue, the endearing fallibility of human hands awaken a kinship with these objects that is more enduring, more satisfying than ultimate perfection could ever arouse. Perfection stimulates the senses; imperfection kindles the imagination. A beautiful child fills you with wondering admiration, but a cluster of freckles on his nose will make you want to kiss him. And so it is with these products of Indian hands.

Of course, imperfection must be more than overbalanced by beauty. And function is never enough. But in these arts of the plateau, the use has merely determined the type, which is idealized through size, color, design, shape, texture, ornament. In these objects made by brown hands, humanity is objectified, and therefore beauty is intensified. To evaluate them justly, the cold judgment of the eye must yield to the warm understanding of the heart. Then only can we rightly appreciate them and say with their makers, "In beauty it is finished."

MODERN
PRIMITIVE DESIGNS
OF MEXICO, GUATEMALA AND
THE SOUTHWEST

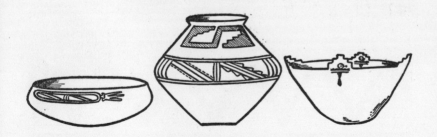

PUEBLO POTTERY DESIGNS AND SHAPES

PUEBLO BASKETRY

Hopi Ceremonial Blanket   Storm clouds, Rain, Lightning

Design from Chief's Blanket

Design from an old Bayeta

Design from old Saddle Blanket

AMERICAN INDIAN TEXTILES

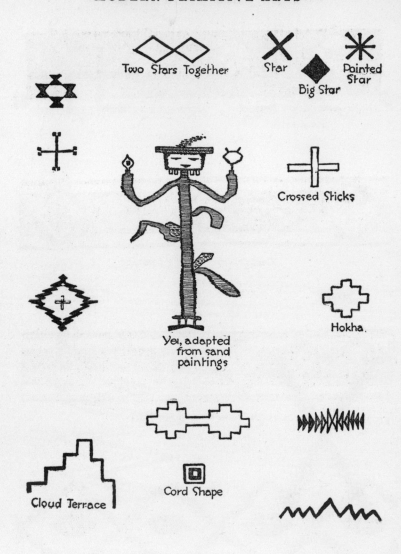

Two Stars Together

Star

Big Star

Pointed Star

Crossed Sticks

Yei, adapted from sand paintings

Hokha.

Cloud Terrace

Cord Shape

AMERICAN INDIAN TEXTILE DESIGNS

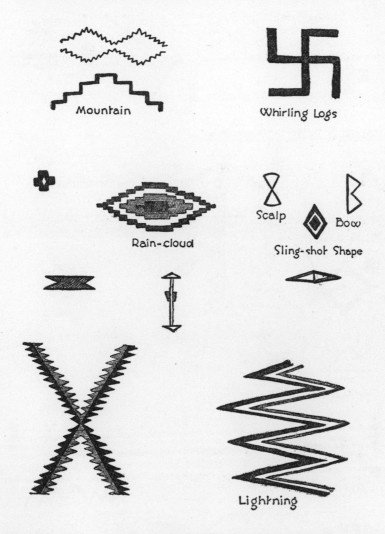

Mountain

Whirling Logs

Rain-cloud

Scalp

Bow

Sling-shot Shape

Lightning

AMERICAN INDIAN TEXTILE DESIGNS

BORDERS

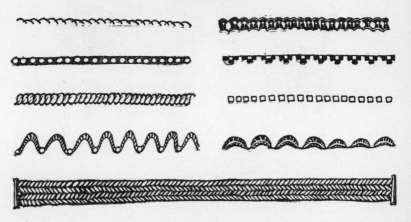

SYMBOLS

Morning Star Moon   Sun   Storm   4 Ages   Cyclone

Horse   Turtle   Rocks   Saddle-bags   Snakes   Lizard   Swallow

Seed-pods   Pine-cone

NAVAHO SILVER

204

FORMS

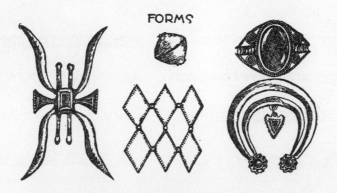

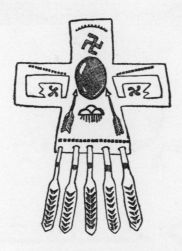

NAVAHO SILVER

Small Chest top and two ends

MEXICAN LACQUER

MEXICAN LACQUER

207

MEXICAN POTTERY DESIGNS AND SHAPES

Border of Ayate

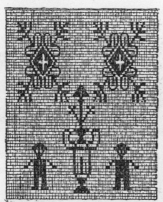

Design from an Ayate

An Otomi Belt

Embroidery from Tolucca

MEXICAN TEXTILE DESIGNS

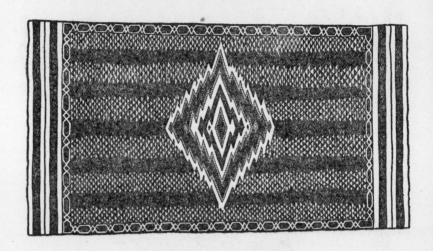

MEXICAN ZERAPES

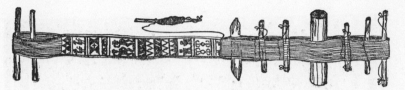

Belt on Loom

Yoke of Huipil

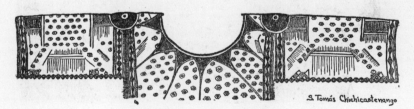

S. Tomás Chichicastenango

Huipil, Sun Emblem

GUATEMALAN TEXTILE DESIGNS

Ants   Double Headed Eagle
                  "Kablicox"

Dogs

GUATEMALAN TEXTILE DESIGNS

Calendar of

Ceremonies, Fiestas, and Markets

Among the Indians, church ceremonies and fiestas are celebrated and markets are held simultaneously. These occasions offer the best opportunities to see their popular arts. Therefore, I have tried to make as complete a calendar as possible, which I hope will guide you in your travels in search of modern primitive arts.

MEXICO

January 1–7	Jojutla, Morelos	New Year's fair
	Tizimin, Yucatan	New Year's fair
January 6	Los Reyes, Mexico	Three Wise Men
January 15	Tenango, Mexico	Religious fair

January 17–25	Leon, Guanajuata	Anniversary of founding the City
February 1–7	Tzintzuntzan	Religious fair
February	Vera Cruz Mazatlan Guanajuata Huejotzingo	Carnival
February 12–19	Chalma	Pilgrimage and fair
February 15–22	Amecameca	Pilgrimage and fair
March 4–13	Taxco	Festival, fair in honor of the True Cross
Easter	From Friday to Monday, celebrated everywhere	Passion plays, flagellants
April 25	San Marcos and many rural towns	Day of St. Mark—Fair
May 1–4	Amatlan de los Reyes, Vera Cruz	Festival, fair
May 1–8	Acapulco	Festival, fair
May 5		Civil holiday everywhere
Corpus Christi	Morelia Puebla Mexico City	Fair
June 10–20	Calpulalpan, Tlaxcala	Festival
July 8–16	Motul, Yucatan	Madonna of Carmel
July 16	Oaxaca	Contests, games
July 24	Torreon	St. James Mystery Plays
August 1–6	Satillo	Festival, fair Christ of the Chapel
August 1–15	Cadereyta near Monterrey	Bullfights, etc.

August 2–9	Tulancingo, Hidalgo	Madonna of the Angels—Dances, cockfights, music
August 8–22	San Lorenzo	St. Lawrence
August 10–20	Amozoc	Madonna of the Assumption
September 1–8	Los Remedios Tepozitan	Madonna and Harvest; Madonna of Nativity and El Tepozteco
September 1–30	Matamoros	Festival season
September 5–15	Zacatecas	Madonna
September 10–20	Chihuahua	National Independence
September 16	Celebrated everywhere	National Independence Day Fair in Mexico City
September 24 to October 8	Magadelena	St. Francis Xavier—Fair, dances, mystery plays, races
September 27 to October 14	Merida	Christ of the Blisters—Dances, parades
October 1–12	Pachuca	St. Francis of Assisi
October 4–12	Zapopan	Madonna of Zapocan—Fair
October 10	Tlacolula, Oaxaca	Dance of the Feathers
October 30 to November 2	All Mexico Open-air market in Mexico City	Most important fiesta of the year—Day of the Dead
November 1–10	Colima	All Soul's Fair—Dances, fireworks, bullfights
November 3–12	San Martin Texmelucan	St. Martin—Dances, ceremonies, cockfights, roses
November 25 to December 16	Patzcuaro	Madonna of Health—Dances, bullfights
December 1–10	Compostela	Lord of Mercy—Native dances, rodeos, bullfights
December 3–13	Mexico	Virgin of Guadalupe—Pilgrimages to Guadalupe shrine

December 5–15	Iguala	Horse fair, bullfights
December 1–10	Puente de Ixtla, Morelos	Immaculate Conception—Mystery plays, dances
December 8–14	Tuxtla Gutierrez, Chiapas	Virgin of Guadalupe
December 12–16	Monterrey	Virgin of Guadalupe—Festival, fair
December 15 to January 6	Tuxtepec, Oaxaca	Christmas festival
December 1 to January 6	Christmas season celebrated in Mexico City, Celaya, and Queretaro	

NEW MEXICO

February 23	San Ildefonso	Deer dance
March	San Ildefonso	Bull dance
May 1	San Felipe	St. Phillip's Day
June 13	Sandia	St. Anthony's Day
June 24	San Juan	St. John's Day Tablita dance
July 14	Cochiti	St. Bonaventure's Day—Corn dance
July 26	Santa Ana	Fiesta
August 2	Jemez	Our Lady of the Angels
August 4	Santa Domingo	Corn ceremony
August 10	Picuris	Fiesta
August 12	Santa Clara	Corn and rain dance
August 15	Zia	Assumption of the Blessed Virgin

CEREMONIES, FIESTAS, AND MARKETS

August 28	Isleta	St. Augustine's Day—fiesta
August	Gallup	Intertribal dance
September	Santa Fé	Fiesta and Southwestern Indian fair
September 2	Acoma	Annual fiesta and dance
September 4	Isleta	Fiesta
September 6	San Ildefonso	Harvest dance
September 19	Laguna	Annual fiesta and dance
September 30	Taos	San Geronimos' Day
October 4	Nambe, Santa Fé	St. Francis' Day
November 12	Tesuque	San Diego's Day
November 12	Jemez	San Diego's Day—Harvest and corn dance
November 30	Zuñi	Saint Andrew's Day
Early December	Zuñi	"Shalako" ceremonies
December 24	Santa Domingo	Deer dance
December 24	Most villages have dances after midnight mass.	

ARIZONA PUEBLOS

January	Buffalo dance
February	Powamu—Bean sprouting
March	Palululong—Plumed serpent
April May June	Katcina ceremonies

August	Snake and antelope ceremonies
September	Lagon basket dance
October	Maran and Oagol basket dance, odd-numbered years
November	New fire ceremony
December	Sagalina—Winter solstice

Bibliography

THE RIO GRANDE PUEBLOS

The American Indian by Clark Wissler, Oxford University Press, New York.

Indian Blankets and Their Makers by George Wharton James, Tudor Publishing Co., New York.

Dancing Gods by Erna Fergusson, Alfred A. Knopf, New York.

First Penthouse Dwellers of America by Ruth M. Underhill, J. J. Augustin, New York.

The Romance of Archeology by R. V. D. Magoffin and Emily C. Davis, Garden City Publishing Company, Garden City.

Indians of the Southwest by Pliny Earle Goddard, American Museum of Natural History, New York.

Navajo Shepherd and Weaver by Gladys A. Reichard, J. J. Augustin, New York.

Native Tales of New Mexico by Frank G. Applegate, J. B Lippincott Company, Philadelphia.

Indians of the Northwest Coast by Pliny Earle Goddard, American Museum of Natural History, New York.

Indians of the Plains by Clark Wissler, American Museum of Natural History, New York.

The Indians of the Enchanted Mesa—Hopi and Navajo by Leo Crane, Little, Brown & Company, Boston.

The Indian's Book by Natalie Curtis (Brorlin), Harper & Brothers, New York.

Pueblo Pottery-Making—A Study of the Village of San Ildefonso by Carl E. Guthe, Yale University Press, New Haven.

Indian Basketry by George Wharton James, Henry Malkan, New York.

The Santa Fé Trail by R. L. Duffus, Tudor Publishing Co., New York.

The Element of Terror in Primitive Art by Barr Ferree, Pepper Collection.

Universal Indian Sign Language by William Tomkins, Frye and Smith, San Diego.

Books of the Southwest—A General Bibliography by Mary Tucker, J. J. Augustin, New York.

Navaho Silversmiths by Washington Matthews, Bureau of Ethnology, Second Annual Report, 1880–81.

MEXICO

Your Mexican Holiday by Anita Brenner, G. P. Putnam's Sons, New York.

Fiesta in Mexico by Erna Fergusson, Alfred A. Knopf, New York.

Idols Behind Altars by Anita Brenner, Harcourt, Brace & Co., New York.

Majolica of Mexico by Edwin Atlee Barber, Pennsylvania Museum of Art, Philadelphia.

Mornings in Mexico by D. H. Lawrence, Alfred A. Knopf, New York.

BIBLIOGRAPHY

Mexico and Its Heritage by Ernest Gruening, D. Appleton-Century Co. Inc., New York.

Little Mexico by William Spratling, Jonathan Cape & Harrison Smith, New York.

Prologue to Mexico by Marian Storm, Alfred A. Knopf, New York.

"The Land of the Pheasant and the Deer" by Antonio Mediz Bolio, Editorial, *Cultura*, Mexico.

Mexico, A Study of Two Americans by Stuart Chase, The Macmillan Company, New York.

The Emily Johnston De Forrest Collection of Mexican Majolica, The Metropolitan Museum of Art, New York.

The First Half Century of Spanish Dominion in Mexico by The Rev. Francis Borgia Stech, Central Bureau Press, St. Louis.

Artists and Craftsmen in Ancient Central America by George C. Vaillant, American Museum of Natural History, New York.

Mexican Folkways, edited and published by Frances Toor, Mexico City.

The Aztecs, Their History, Manners and Customs by Lucien Biart, Dodd, Mead & Company Inc., New York.

The Story of Mexico by Helen Ward Banks, Frederick A. Stokes Company, New York.

Viva Mexico! by Charles Macomb Flandrau, D. Appleton-Century Co. Inc., New York.

The True Story of the Conquest of Mexico by Bernal Diaz del Castillo, Robert McBride Company, New York.

Cuatemo by Cora Walker, The Dayton Press, New York.

GUATEMALA

Guatemala by Erna Fergusson, Alfred A. Knopf, New York.

Images of Earth: Guatemala by Agnes Rothery, The Viking Press, New York.

Notes on a Drum by Joseph Henry Jackson, The Macmillan Company, New York.

"Through the Marvelous Highlands of Guatemala," reprinted from October, 1917 issue of the *Bulletin of the Pan-American Union*, Washington Government Printing Office.

Guatemala Textiles by Lilly de Jough Osborne, Department of Middle American Research, Tulane University, New Orleans, 1935.

The Year Bearer's People by Oliver La Farge, Tulane University, New Orleans.

A Glimpse at Guatemala—Some Notes on Ancient Monuments by A. C. and A. P. Maudslay, J. Murray, London.

Guide Book to the Ruins of Quirigua by Sylvannus G. Morley, Carnegie Institution, Washington.

Travels in Guatemala and Central America by John L. Stephens, Harper & Brothers, New York.

Maria Paluna by Blair Niles, Longmans, Green & Company, New York.

Sparks Fly Upward by Oliver La Farge, Houghton Mifflin Company, Boston.

Banana Gold by Carleton Beals, J. B. Lippincott Company, Philadelphia.

The Romance and Rise of the American Tropics by Samuel Crowther, Doubleday, Doran & Company, Inc., New York.

Index

223